out of print

15 –

GOOD TASTE COSTS NO MORE

Good Taste

Costs No More

BY RICHARD GUMP

Doubleday & Company, Inc.

Garden City, New York, 1951

To Agnes

Acknowledgments

The author is greatly indebted

    to Ross B. Wills for his interest and expert advice,

    to Ben Davis for his experienced help,

    to Gerhardt Hurt for his eloquent cartoons,

    to Skelton Studios for many of the photographs in the text,

    to The Metropolitan Museum of Art,

    to The Cooper Union Museum for the Arts of Decoration,

    to The Library of The Cooper Union Museum for the Arts of
      Decoration,

    to Knoll Associates, Inc.,

    and to many others for their kind co-operation.

Contents

GOOD TASTE COSTS NO MORE

The Gilt Complex

It all started when the late George Cro-Magnon had sense enough to come in out of the rain. That first abode was purely functional. But one day the little woman found a ledge in the cave and stuck something up there. When the old man dragged the dinner in that night, she wanted to know if he noticed something different. He did, and in rather a belligerent tone asked, "What's *that?*"

"It's a rock," she answered, and with commendable control refrained from adding, "you dumb ape."

"What's it for?" he wanted to know.

"It looks pretty," she replied firmly.

He stared at it for a moment, shrugged, and said, "When do we eat?" And that, one might suppose, was that.

But human nature being what it is, presently everyone was

thrashing about in the underbrush and coming up with that curious bone or rock that added a certain something to the Paleolithic décor. And as more and more of these folks crawled out of the primeval ooze, got up off all fours and put something on the mantelpiece, variations occurred and inevitably comparisons were made.

"I don't see why *she* has a musk-ox horn over her bed when I haven't even got a bed!"

"My dear, did you notice that ridiculous mammoth tusk in their squatting place?"

"If you call a saber-toothed tiger skin good taste, *well!*"

Already the thing was out of hand. Everyone was trying to impress everyone else. Taste was born. And civilization, with its inescapable and frightening implications, was upon us.

Now we are up to our necks in the Twentieth Century. The menagerie has become the ménage. And George's descendants are daily more concerned with the things that add a certain something to the Cenozoic décor.

But today the little woman doesn't just say, "It looks pretty," and let it go at that. For she has been told with heavy significance, *ad repetatum*, in every advertising medium known to modern man, that it is smart to "Steep Your Home in Tradition," that it must be "Functionally Styled for Today's Living." She is told to "Bring the Outside Inside" and vice versa. Her ears ring with phrases like, "Truly Possessions of Personal Pride," "Period Magic in the Modern Manner," and "High Style of Modern Baroque."

I make my living trying to give the public what it wants. And with a personal experience of more than twenty-five years, in a family business over ninety years old, engaged in designing, buying, and selling the things that go to make a house a home, I am convinced that "What the Public Wants" seldom is determined by the public but by the "trade"—manufacturers, promotion experts, factory salesmen, and buyers for the stores—all, more or less, irresponsibly experimenting with the market. It is not surprising that often the public's recognition of the desirable is either a case of mistaken identity or a happy accident. It follows that millions are wasted yearly by the public on things they wouldn't want if they knew better.

There is no doubt that the level of taste is steadily rising, that more and more people are becoming conscious of the nature and the value of good design, that there's a growing understanding of how to get your money's worth, and that people are less impressed by ostentation and affectation. There are stacks of fine books on art, decorating, and design, read by an increasing number. There is a generous choice of material on the subject in the editorial sections of a few conscientious magazines devoted to the house and its appointments. But as a merchant dealing with manufacturers, salesmen, buyers, salespeople, and customers, I am reminded every day of the confusion and nonsense that obscure the view of the worth-while and the desirable.

This book is an attempt from the other side of the counter to offer a few suggestions to the enthusiastic homemaker and the chap who foots the bills—not only how to get your money's worth, but more for your money; to offer a simple approach toward an honest selection of things for the home; to discriminate between market value and esthetic value; to point out that esthetic value is within the reach of everyone and should be the paramount consideration in making any purchase; to show, in short, that good taste costs no more.

Whose good taste? Yours, mine, anybody's. Any definition of good taste in absolute terms is, of course, an absurdity. There are exceptions to nearly every rule which might be used to identify it, and learning the exceptions is no solution. The exceptions to the exceptions make the recognition of good taste seem as unlikely as a mole leading a blind man.

But from all ages there are things that have survived the test of time. Some of these things were admired in their day; many were not. Today we find them beautiful. Some of the things of our own age will endure and be desirable a hundred years from now. It is not the critic of the time who finally determines the success or failure of a design, but the old fellow with the scythe whose judgment prevails. The backward look then is easy. And since there are certain standards of excellence from all periods, they suggest a means of identifying and recognizing good taste from the viewpoint of the present.

. . . his judgment prevails . . .

What forms the public's choice of personal possessions? Considerations widely believed important in determining the worth of an object offered for sale are its age, the material used, the time consumed in manufacture, where it was made, how it was made, its costliness, to whom it belonged, and its elaborateness. Observe a certain antique carving of ornate design, made of a precious material which took years to fashion and was once in the possession of a notorious ruler. But what have you? Yet many people exclaim over its beauty. Why? They are awed by the preciousness of the material, they are impressed by its long survival, they are dazzled by its intricacy, the exotic place of its origin, the travail of its manufacture, the fame of its former owner, and the fact that only a solvent spendthrift could afford it.

Our standards of what makes a thing valuable are generally wrong. We do not know how to judge the merit, desirability, the value of the things with which we spend our lives. We lose sight of one simple consideration, without which everything else is meaningless. Is IT GOOD-LOOK-ING? Is it beautiful, does it appeal to the esthetic sense, is it well designed, does it delight the eye?

Is it good-looking? This is generally the last thing people consider and many times do not consider at all, although they think they do. Is this some form of general myopia? Surely not in a country whose exploitation of physical beauty has influenced the taste of the world, whose fashions make Americans, as a mass, better dressed than any other people, whose machines, household wares, and some of its architecture compete in honesty of design, good looks, and utility with the best in the world.

. . . only a solvent spendthrift could afford it . . .

Why are we particularly impressed by age? As a people with a short national history are we fascinated by the romance of antiquity? Whatever the reason, all too often the old is automatically considered valuable. Whether in Post Street, San

. . . the shopper will give it a double take . . .

Francisco, or the Rue Bonaparte, Paris, if the salesman can say, "This is two hundred years old," the American shopper will give it a double take and often enough buy it!

About once each week the same scene, more or less, takes place. Someone brings in an object that has been "in the family for over a hundred years" and "is worth a great deal of money." In most cases, and with as much delicacy as possible, they must be told that it is worth nothing to a dealer because it isn't good-looking. "But it's an antique," they insist. They do not realize that age can express beauty very well but may have nothing to do with it. Whether a bowl was made two thousand years ago or flew off the production line last Tuesday is immaterial. It may or may not be good-looking, and age won't determine that.

There are a few valid reasons for revering age. Certain antiques or ancient art works have a visual stimulus, a message, a certain characteristic beauty that is associated in our minds with the periods of history from which they stem. Their identity and age seem nearly indivisible. But it is their *characteristic beauty* that is the main reason for their being of value, not the time of

. . . authentic T'ang sculpture of great artistic value . . .

their creation. For example, it would be hard to find things of more artistic worth than some of the sculptures of the T'ang dynasty made in China over a thousand years ago. But when collectors or dealers conclude sweepingly that everything of this period is great, they are assuming that antiquity and value go hand in hand. It is far better to own a nobly conceived modern sculpture, at a tenth the price, than an ill-conceived authentic T'ang piece.

Happily, there are times when artistic expression has achieved and sustained greatness. One does not see a poor Archaic Greek sculpture, an inferior Byzantine mosaic, or seldom a bad thirteenth-century Limoges enamel.

. . . a nobly conceived modern sculpture . . .

Unhappily, we have the antithesis. When we look at the sad-saccharine works of Guido Reni, Carlo Dolci, and some of their seventeenth-century Italian contemporaries, we realize how bad they are. But some of the most unforgettable characters we've ever met stand before this sentimental rubbish choking with emotion. "Weren't the Old Masters wonderful!" They have been seduced by the popular misconception that age is synonymous with value. And surely, since they are old, therefore valuable, it *must* follow that they are good-looking. It is not age that makes a work of art or adds to its intrinsic value, although it is often an excuse for inflating its market value.

There are certain magic words that anesthetize the average

19

customer. The potency of some is well understood—gold, silver, jade, diamond, crystal, ivory. They have an intrinsic value, and few substitutes are as desirable for the purposes to which they are suited. The fact that they are and often have been misused can be shown by many unbelievable examples. But even so, precious, unusual, and merely obscure materials hypnotize the public. Do they suggest wealth? Prestige? Whatever the reasons, if one can say, "This chair is made of genuine abaca-dabra wood," a glint often appears in the customer's eye that wasn't there when he saw a better-looking, stronger chair of ordinary birch at half the price.

There is a general admiration for things that have been a long time in the making. Are we bored with the rigid perfection of the machine? Are we awed and charmed by the quiet way of life that allows years for the painstaking task of making one unique thing? Whatever the reasons, most of us are thunderstruck to think that it took a whole family (and families were large in those days) twenty-five years to make a Tabriz rug. There are four hundred knots to the square inch, and though it can offend the eye as brutally as a modern machine-made imitation, the ordeal of its fabrication awakens the desire to possess it. Certainly such a thing is interesting; you wonder what family quirk or tribal custom caused this quarter-century fixation, and what the incidence of astigmatism must have been.

The mention that certain articles are "imported" enhances their importance in the eyes of the public. Anything from somewhere else seems, ipso facto, desirable. If a saddle blanket was brought from the uplands of Afghanistan via Tibet by natives suffering a diet of yak

. . . anything from somewhere else seems desirable . . .

butter, it arouses special interest, although a second look may make us ask if this trip was necessary. Why are we excited by things made in alien lands? Why are we so often ready to open our checkbooks in a more co-operative spirit for something with a foreign stamp than a vase, chair, or rug made in the United States?

Maybe we have been impressed by foreign opinion that we are uncultured, crass materialists. We have been a rich relation treated like a poor relation, a little vulgar, a little embarrassing to have around, but useful for picking up the chit.

Our European cousins have considered us perhaps clever in our own strange way but without charm and sadly lacking in the refinements of life and living. Now, after the debacle of World War II, the opinion is much the same, but the attitude is changing. It is bright on our side of the Atlantic, dull on theirs. Our fortunate geographic position, wide natural resources, great productive capacity, and varied skills have come to full bloom in the mid-twentieth century.

Our metamorphosis from wilderness to world power has been swift, and we've had to pick up what culture we could hastily en route. At the turn of the century the fortunate few were making the grand tour and bringing back an indiscriminate collection of European objects to enhance the home. It was the fashion to show stereopticon slides of the wonders they'd seen and have a "gathering" to tell the less fortunate about the trip. Their daughters studied "French," the unsoundness of which investment would be proven eventually by the total incomprehension of the first Parisian taxi driver the girls encountered. However, travel was broadening, culture was refining, and if you couldn't get it first hand, well, there were other ways. Each vernal equinox found buyers in every factory

and studio of Europe. Back home the customers liked busts of Dante, marble preferred; "genuine" Italian Capo da Monte, made in Germany; odd-shaped vases with hand-painted rural scenes touched here and there with gold. And everyone just *had* to have a Limoges china set! They bought the Gladiator, dying in bronze—and other sculptures "dramatic" and "sensitive"; pictures that "told a story"; oil lamps in verdigris standing on cloven hoofs; Dutch silver pock-marked with *repoussé* windmills; and Swiss wood tortured into hatracks and clocks. And to contain knickknacks, vitrines in *vernis Martin* with Watteau scenes painted on the front and lined with fine brocade.

You could buy oil paintings by the yard and specify your favorite subject. One prominent dowager said she wouldn't sit for a famous American portraitist but would wait until she went to Europe to be painted by "one of the Old Masters."

Much of the loot from these forays remains in present-day houses—"heirlooms," they're called—and the dear little cachepot that Grandma picked up in Brussels is something that will influence granddaughter's taste, for good or ill. If she is wising up she'll rebel and indeed cache it away and only bring it out

when Grandma calls. If not, she'll value it as highly as the Spanish shawl that Mama brought from China to festoon the piano.

"It's a complex fate being an American," as Henry James said, "and one of the responsibilities it entails is fighting a superstitious valuation of Europe." At the turn of the century European influence on United States culture was far stronger than it is today; we have digested and assimilated some of it and discarded, ignored, and forgotten much of it. But enough of its influence remains as a hangover to keep us dragging our feet in our muddled wanderings toward a culture of our own.

Foreign countries are as adept as we are in confecting junk, but well-chosen imports greatly enrich the selection in our stores and the attractiveness of our houses. In certain fields of art and manufacture the market abroad is supreme. When it is cut off we notice that we are deprived of much that is desirable. There are many special products that have been made and perfected for hundreds of years in scores of foreign factories and workshops which we cannot match. Either we lack the special skill, sometimes handed down for generations, or our machine-geared setup and higher scale of living make the manufacture of these handicrafts impractical. But whether it is Venetian, Swedish, or Irish glass; French, Belgian, or Italian lace; Chinese, Japanese, German, or French porcelain; a Turkish, African, or Persian rug; if it is not well designed and good to look at, it is not worth buying.

Suppose you are told, "This fabric is woven only in the waters of the Gulf of Hoplandia at 63 degrees Fahrenheit

. . . woven only in Hoplandia . . .

during the third day of the monsoon." This may all be quite true, but unless the article justifies this startling custom by being uniquely good-looking, you should counter with a quiet, "So what?" The fact that an object was made in an archaic or out-of-ordinary way is many times allowed to govern the question of its esthetic worth. The hand does not necessarily express artistry any better than the machine. The real value of the machine-made or the hand-made depends upon whose hand makes the unique article or whose hand does the sketch for the production line. If the designer is good, the product should be good. Our surprised admiration is occasionally justified when we see something fine that is hand-made, hand-carved, hand-embroidered, hand-painted. But if we let ourselves believe that method means more than modest beauty, the forest will be lost among the trees and we won't see decorative art with an appraising eye. We'll see an Indian in the Painted Desert instead of the blanket, an old lady with failing eyesight in Burano instead of the lace table mats, a Chinese in a dim shop in Peking instead of the jade bowl.

. . . hand-blown glass is made today .

Obviously there are many things that can be made only in unusual ways. After trying many modern tools, machine- and hand-driven, the Chinese found that there was but one way to carve jade. And until the Japanese invasion the artisans on Jade Street, Peking, were still employing the old-fashioned wire saws, flat metal disks, and wheels driven by foot treadle, a

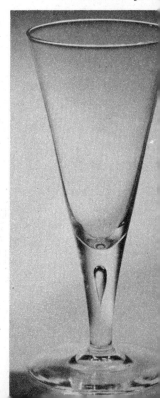

Steuben Glass, Inc.

method thousands of years old. Any considerable design in this material is bound to take a great many man-hours of skilled effort. Although types and qualities differ, American, Venetian, Mexican, or any hand-blown glass is made today essentially as it was in Marco Polo's time. This old process seems rude and primitive but it has proved to be the superior way. There have

. . . as it was in Marco Polo's time . . .

been a few minor changes, but the hand loom remains much the same as it was long ago. An Inca native, Azerbaijan shepherdess, or art-school apprentice goes through the same age-old motions in the process of weaving. The potter's wheel still spins as it always has. Hand-wrought silver has changed little in centuries. Engraving has not altered in our progressive age. Techniques vary, but the method of painting in oils is hardly different now from that of Van Dyck's day. When we say hand embroidery we are also being specific. No machine at present is facile enough to reproduce the quality of designs that can be done by hand.

The legend of the machine-monster swamping us with monstrosities isn't necessarily so. There are very few times when we

25

must resort to expensive hand-woven fabrics to get a desired effect. The textures, colors, and variety of materials and designs made by today's mills can usually meet any demand. The few exceptions are unusual textures and color combinations for special effects. Usually, printed fabrics to please anyone's taste can be found on the market. Certainly, if an allover design is used, it is sensible to buy it ready-made. But if unusual spacing of pattern is needed, it must be hand done by silk screen or special blocking.

The biggest bull in the china shop is the nonsense about fine, hand-painted china. Under this careless classification are tons of patterns more fit for a shooting gallery than a pleasant fireside. China outlasts earthenware and pottery; hand painting can be more effective than decal reproduction, but the extra expense is justified only if the design is good.

A machine can produce more spoon bowls in a week than a skilled silversmith can hammer out in years. It can also stamp the hammer marks on the spoon bowl if its masters go in for that kind of chicanery. Up to the middle of the eighteenth century the wealthy carried their silver flatware with them while away from home. Only the rich could own such a luxury, and they were determined to enjoy it to the full. Today, in our remarkable mechanized country, nearly everyone can have a set of flat silver or a good substitute. It is probably the first household requisite that nesting couples think about. If they're close to the norm they'll pick out something florid and intricate. They'll be told, "Notice the fineness of design." Stamped out by the thousands, it has far less claim to fineness than the delicate parts manufactured for scientific instruments. Because they are senselessly overdecorated,

. . . the wealthy carried their silver with them . . .

the knives, forks, and spoons needed for basic utility are uncomfortable and clumsy to use. The best-selling flatware pattern in the country is typical. It is elaborate and awkward, but its success is the envy of the trade. There are some sensible designs, pleasant to use, but they are not the biggest sellers. Good new designs seldom appear on the market. The manufacturers have no philanthropic urge to invest a fortune in new dies while the old ones sell so well. One factory owner has several splendid patterns on ice. If he made them he would have to use them to eat his own words. They are so simple and superior to the intricate tomfooleries he has been producing and promoting for years.

. . . pistol-grip knives and typical spoon and fork of the 18th century

When we look at the pistol-grip knife and typical spoon and fork of the eighteenth century we see that their fine, basic simplicity has not been bested in later designs. They are as suitable in a modern house as in the period setting of their time. Any patterns as good as these lose nothing by being manufactured in quantity for everyday use.

Designed by John Van Koert for Towle Mfg. Co.

. . . a modern design equal to the best of the 18th century . . .

Cut-crystal stemware is generally supposed to be desirable. Cutting runs up the cost of any glass but sometimes runs down its appearance. Both the designer and cutter are tempted to see how far they can go with complicated patterns which often detract from the shape of the glass. Although this takes skill of a sort, the result, flashing with refracted light, is a jarring note on any table. There is plenty of good-looking cut glass. It is distinguished by graceful, simple designs that don't destroy basic form, that don't feel like a nest of nettles when you pick them up.

Since the artist's talent is often inadequate, there are masses of monstrous oils that are admired on the basis of the labor that has gone into them. Many of them are so tiresome to look at that the only idea that occurs to most of us is, "Think of all that 'hand' work, wonder how long it took."

A true artist does not belabor his public with the painstaking effort and study necessary to produce his work. We know that Rembrandt was a great technician and a tormented man. But when we see one of his best canvases we feel power and inspiration, not weeks of hard, sad labor. Beethoven and Wagner lift us into their supreme world. Their music is an emotional and intellectual experience, not a lesson in diatonics. The best art of the Ming dynasty, 1368 to 1644, and later use of the same technique, gives a feeling of spontaneous inspiration. We would not suspect that the ability to produce this fresh

. . . a fresh and perfect impression by T'ang Yin, 1470–1523

and perfect impression with a few strokes of a brush comes only after years of hard work combined with fine talent. A good water color strikes the same note; it seems dashed off in a carefree moment, with a magic result. It is not the medium that makes a worth-while picture. Because of the materials and technique involved, it takes a longer time to produce an oil painting than a water color or drawing. But the artist working in oils can make mistakes and alterations that would ruin a water color. It is a foolish pretense to think that an oil painting is better, assuming both are of the same caliber. Yet this attitude is so popular with the dealers and public that if you are in the market for a really "good picture," it is taken for granted that it must be compounded of canvas and oils. The benefit arising out of this hocus-pocus is that good pictures in other media are generally modestly priced and the customer can get a better work of art, with more intrinsic and esthetic value, for less money.

An obvious question occurs to Americans when confronted with anything new—a house, battleship, or jewel—"How much did it cost?" We've been kidded and criticized for this curiosity all over the world. Perhaps other peoples are more subtle than we are, but you can be sure the question occurs just as often to any of them. And since money of some kind is the basis of exchange for all countries, it is an eminently sensible question. You can be equally sure that when something takes the eye of an African tribesman he quickly translates it into wives or other chattels.

There are many times when knowing the price will suggest a fair idea of value. But in the field of esthetics it's a pretty shaky indicator. Suppose you are well-heeled enough to announce, "I'm redoing my whole house. Money's no object. I want the best." And the decorators move in, or you decide to handle it yourself. Sometime later the job is done and you assume you got the best. Didn't you spend the most? Maybe you were lucky in your choice of decorator, or knew what you were doing—maybe you did get "the best." But the happy result didn't come about because there was plenty of money to spend. The price tag hints what is "in demand," or what someone fancies is. But if we are shown something that doesn't appeal to us and told that it is priced at four figures, we'll look to see what we missed the first time and probably agree that it is "beautiful." The chances of its being beautiful or beastly are about fifty-fifty, and the hard facts in dollars and cents don't mean a thing.

Before we find ourselves in downward flight with saw, limb, and all, we must consider rarities, the freaks and eccentrics in the world of art. There are several reasons for objects becoming rare. Among them are carelessness—generations of butter-fingers dropping those fine old things that aren't made any more; uncommunicativeness or amnesia—refusing to part with or forgetting the formula for making any number of things; stupidity—making a mistake in something that should be an exact replica and thus creating a curiosity; aggressiveness—overthrowing one civilization in favor of another; the wantonness of nature—destruction by natural causes, and lack of abundance. One of the peccadilloes of *genus homo* is to want something no one else has. When this desire bears fruit, we have the collector. And the things in scarce supply, for the reasons mentioned, are what he and his fellow collectors vie for, so the price goes up. Sometimes a rarity has little or no esthetic value, and the friend who would have you admire a visual embarrassment of this kind might as well hang those certificates of

. . . a pertinent example worth a lot of money . . .

. . . any room would be better off with this . . .

U. S. Steel Preferred on the wall for the enjoyment of his guests. There is a highboy in the Metropolitan Museum which is a pertinent example. It is worth a lot of money, but any room would be better off with a simple cherrywood piece for a fraction of the price. The Victoria and Albert Museum in London has a fine collection of clinkers by Chippendale. They are excellent examples of period and craftsmanship. As documents they are intriguing. As designs they are extremely unlikely.

But there are rarities of great value that are equally valuable esthetically. Their appeal is timeless and their beauty is of such import that as standards of excellence of any age they will survive as long as they exist. Holbein portraits, Dürer woodcuts and engravings, Ingres drawings, most examples of fifteenth-century Italian and Flemish painting, early Christian glass, and Cézanne water colors are in this class. And cheeringly enough, rarities like these which please the eye are, through the years, a safe investment, while those which are not distinguished for their good looks often decrease in value.

Clinkers by Chippendale:

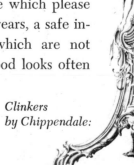

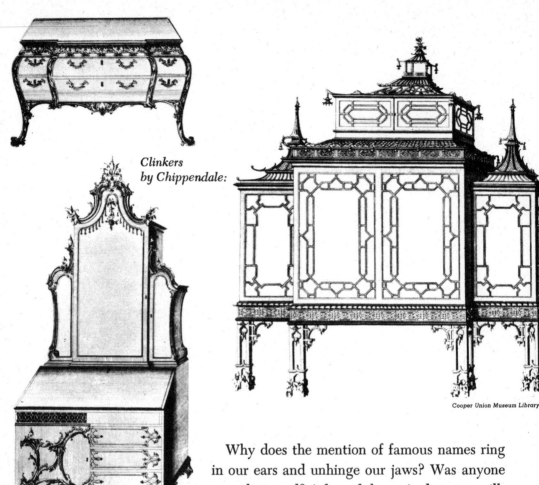

Clinkers by Chippendale:

Cooper Union Museum Library

Why does the mention of famous names ring in our ears and unhinge our jaws? Was anyone ever that good? A few of them. And we are willing to say that they are above criticism. We will differ about whose are the places of honor, but we would see them together in the same company. Botticelli, Rembrandt, Vermeer, Cézanne, Turner, Phidias, Michelangelo, Paul Revere, Leonardo da Vinci, Manet, to pull a few out of a well-worn hat. Their works were masterful and nearly always a masterpiece. But most artists had their inspired moments and their bad days.

Any picture dealer or alert gallery-goer knows that the work of nearly every well-known artist is not uniform. And though the name is A-1, the painting may be 4-F. A poor Rubens would be easy to sell because the excellence of his best work is so universally appreciated it even spreads an aura of desirability over his potbellied potboilers. A dealer can hook the poor fish with a famous name as bait. But even a clever dealer cannot sell an inferior picture for nearly as much as he can demand for a fine example. An art expert will always qualify the canvas. If it has little to recommend it but its creator, he may say, "I believe this to be an authentic Gainsborough, probably painted in Ipswich." But if the picture is excellent, he will add, "This is a splendid example of his portraiture," so inferring that the name has a certain value but that a particularly fine painting by Gainsborough is worth a great deal more.

An artist is hardly his own best judge. If he were, there would be more works of art and fewer pieces of taxidermy masquerading as the real thing. His feeble efforts would be destroyed and his best vein exploited. Gallery-goers are pleased when they can recognize a painter by his work, so they judge a picture by the artist who painted it. If one spots an Utrillo, an easy mark, he will buy it in preference to a better canvas by a lesser-known painter. A dealer will not discourage this habit because well-known names sell for higher prices. But a connoisseur will look for a good painting first and consider the artist's name second; his judgment is sophisticated and he is interested in quality and discovery. It is unfortunate that the average buyer is not aware that it is better in every way to own an excellent Bassano, for instance, than a poor Tintoretto.

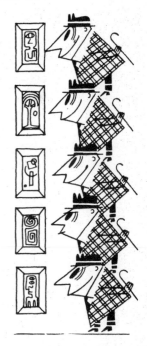

. . . Boule cabinet, a collector's item . . .

*. . . candlesticks
by Paul Lamarie . . .*

A Boule cabinet may be thoroughly certified, as today we think its maker should have been. It is a collector's item with its weird use of tortoise shell and brass over a malformed shape dripping with useless appendages. Collectors look for names, marks, pedigrees, brands, and labels. A dealer makes an easy pitch when he says, "This is genuine Sèvres," or, "Notice the mark. This urn is by Jacob Petit." Too seldom does he offer the collector something beautiful that happens to have the mark of the period. Candlesticks by Paul Lamarie will bring a big price. They may be an overdone design, but the collector, in his worship of the silver calf, looks only for the correct hallmark. If we could own an original by Paul Revere, an authentic Queen Anne sugar shaker or George I coffeepot, we would have a sound investment in excellent design as well as a collector's item of aristocratic pedigree.

It would be pleasant to own a work by Cellini. Its resale to a great collector or museum would buy a comfortable annuity. Benvenuto was a wizard of a technician, a superb artist, and sometimes merely a crafty artisan. Consider the too-flamboyant design. Is it handsome? Is it *good?*

34

James Robinson, Inc.

. . . a sound investment
. excellent design: right,
een Anne sugar shaker;
George I coffeepot . . .

. . . is it good?

A genuine Gobelin may be a genuine hob-goblin or a gem. If it is a fine tapestry artistically, it will be worth more than one poorly conceived, but the fame of the name alone will guarantee market value and the awed admiration of the public. Picasso has made great contributions to the art of our time. Many of his canvases are desirable to own; others would be completely worthless if his name were not signed to them. A Matisse can mean a great deal or little. His poorer paintings, without his signature, could hardly earn gallery space. Beethoven's "Battle Symphony" is a misfire, and Wagner slipped when he wrote the "Christopher Columbus Overture."

Cellini cup from The Metropolitan Museum of Art

As the real connoisseurs define the value of an artist's work, so should we think of it. First, is it a good work of art? And then, who made it?

Since the days when George Washington was sleeping

35

around, we have been intrigued by things that belonged to famous people. Fondness for the erstwhile possessions of someone else may be born of a documentary fascination and make no sense for beauty's sake. The clock that belonged to Frederick the Great is interesting because he owned it. But is it evidence that Frederick and good taste were intimates? Except for jewels and ornaments of definite worth, it is a waste of time and money to buy anything simply because its former owner was a famous figure.

. . . this belonged to
Frederick the Great . . .

To say that something roughly classified as "a fine piece" belonged to the Duke of St. Albans may give it a background of authenticity, and if it is among the possessions of the descendants of the bastard son of Charles II, they no doubt attach some sentimental importance to it. But its appearance may indicate that though their colorful ancestor had an eye for a well-turned limb when attached to one of mother nature's masterpieces, he could not judge a well-turned leg in walnut. There were some discriminating collectors among the famous, and many of their acquisitions are valuable, as are the possessions of others who happened to live in periods of generally enlightened taste.

Nothing so beguiles the unwary as the elaborate. Nothing is so responsible for offenses against good taste as the overwrought, overworked, overdecorated. But overelaboration of design is notoriously associated with beauty and good looks. It is interesting to speculate on the reasons for this common blunder.

Elaboration of design is not limited to what we are pleased to call our higher civilization. The urge to doodle in wood and stone is as old as George Cro-Magnon. Picture our early relative in an idle moment, carving a crude flower on the handle of his ax. The sloth's head was no more easily split open, but it somehow gave the ax an added significance. Now it was more than utilitarian, and made him feel he was a cut above his fellows.

Through the ages this urge to inflate the ego by outfancying our neighbor has led to infinite embellishment and, inevitably, into intricate nonsense. The ornamental grotesqueries that characterize the reign of Louis XIV were created to stun and amaze the world. Nothing in our time has touched the flabbergasting opulence of that period, with the possible exception of a few theater lobbies. Nothing has approached its magnificent craftsmanship, dazzling display, stupefying impact, and preposterous waste.

. . . flabbergasting opulence created . . .

. . . to stun and amaze the world . . .

As a monumental expression of the glories of kingship, the grandeur of France's most magnificent period, Versailles—its colossal size, acres of decorated ceilings, tons of gold leaf, miles of carving, and endless intricacies of design—is a historical document overwhelming in its excitements. Imagine being His Nibs in a place like this!

And there are aspects that are beautiful: the exterior, immense in scale but dignified and handsome in spite of its great mass; the fountains, their fanciful designs charming against the

. . . imagine being His N in a place like this!

background of noble trees; a niche in one of the rooms, lovely despite the restless sea of design that surrounds it. But it is not art for art's sake, though its craftsmanship is wonderfully artful. Versailles represents the ultimate achievement of Louis's purpose—to glorify Louis. It is not good taste as we think of it. It is to "The King's Taste."

And yet we have been sold on the idea that this magnificent curly-whirly is beautiful. Why is gorgeousness mistaken for good design and gold leaf for good taste? The moppet gazes with enchanted eyes at the palaces, national shrines, and public monuments in his schoolbooks. He learns the achievements of the great men who thus left their mark upon the world. And he is taught to judge their greatness by the impressiveness of their relics, invariably grand and elaborate. When the moppet becomes the man he sees some of these things for himself. The technicolored travelogues come alive, and the foreign guide points with particular pride to the monuments of his country's past glory, always drawing attention to the grandest. Look at that palace! It took fifty years to build and cost ten million bucks! Alas, the modest picturesque farmhouse along the way is forgotten.

. . . the white devil's taste . . .

Thus the historical documents of defunct days become symbols of success. And since success is certainly desirable, so must the trappings of success be desirable. Whether a native looks up to the chief, a subject to the king, a workman to the president of the nuts and bolts factory, it is human nature to aspire to a way of life that is a cut above our fellows.

We see the popularity of overdecoration in all periods of prosperity—when Chippendale was master of the intricate and English commerce was flourishing; when Chinese nineteenth-century monstrosities were a manifestation of the white devils' taste and the wealth of the Cantonese; and at the Philadelphia Centennial of 1876 when America expressed her increasing fortune with a surfeit of proudly presented claptrap.

Philadelphia Centennial claptrap:

The modest means of our early settlers, and their preoccupation with knocking off the native and liberating his land, enforced the use of the simple and basic. To this we owe the excellence of the New England, Pennsylvania Dutch, Shaker and Quaker architecture and furniture, as well as the log cabins, stone houses, and adobes farther west.

The rise of the middle class and distribution of wealth to a wider population, the growth of a general prosperity, creates a huge new income group whose taste is often combined with affectation. In our country the economic recklessness of the twenties and subsequent crash forced a simplification of tastes. A few years later, in a cycle of reviving prosperity, the rise of the cost of labor was responsible for limiting much of the elaborate. Unfortunately, American know-how has managed to circumvent this happy state of affairs by using machines that reproduce the contortions of design, making it possible for the ordinary citizen to have something to "The King's Taste."

We are in sympathy with the sentiment that a man's home is his castle, but . . . Let us spend the evening with Charlie. Good old Charlie; you all know him. Outside, his house is a bit of Devon with a dash of the Alhambra and a subtle suggestion of early Place Pigalle under the arches. We bruise our ankle on the foot scraper, a dachshund rampant, and pull on an old anchor chain. The opening bars of the "Blue Danube" chime through the quiet night. A huge bastille-grilled door swings

. . . modest means enforced the simple and basic . . .

back, and Charlie beams a welcome.

We trip on the matted fringe of the deeply carved living-room rug and stifle a cry of fright as we realize that the Federal mirror opposite is just like the fun house and we really don't look that bad. Mrs. Charlie struggles up from an old Tyrolean sleigh chair, disentangling herself from the train of her hostess gown and her own secret thoughts. Charlie waddles off to conjure up an anesthetic. As the guests deploy themselves about the room, brocade draperies rustle and sigh, their silken lengths billowing in the evening breeze and drooling on the floor. Dresden shepherdesses cavort in frozen grace across the glistening surfaces of the end tables whose little legs itch with carving. There's a sudden hissing sound like a barrelful of rattlesnakes. An early Tojo screen slides back and there's old Charlie, in his South Sea Island bar!

As we sit down to the repast we get a sharp gouge in the vertebra. Whirling to deal with the assailant, we're reassured to see it's only the cupids embracing on the chair back. Forcing our best party grimace, we gaze through a Scotch mist at the table. It is a riotous garden! The candlesticks are entwined with glossy silver leaves; the epergne belches grapes and nectarines; little birds flit through the lace of the tablecloth. The service plates are newly minted with heavily encrusted gold borders, and the silver flatware standing at attention on either side swarms with roses strangling one another. A Swiss bell ringer could run the gamut on the collection of stemware before us, its twinkling crystal alive with cut flowers.

It's a feast. Talk about food! And wine: a different vintage with each rich course, though Charlie passes 'em all up and sticks to hiballs. "Wine, you can have it," Charlie remarks. "Elmsworthy can have it, the old tightwad." Elmsworthy, his neighbor, is Charlie's pet peeve. Next door the Elmsworthy manse, grandly spreading over several lots, is, in a word, Tudor. Tudor-and-no-nonsense-about-it. A superb example of its period, considering it was piled up thousands of miles from where it belongs, hundreds of years after its time. Its library is the town wonder, original Jacobean, torn out of a famous old English landmark. It is here the pipe-organ recitals are given, followed by "a bit of sherry." Charlie says, "Old man Elmsworthy may be the president of the bank and I may be hard up someday, but I'll go out of business before I go through another of those 'affairs' he inflicts on harmless folks."

"How about another hiball?" Charlie asks, changing the subject. We ramble into the den and all sink into the lap of a mammoth divan. Charlie tunes in his big blond TV combo.

Some half dozen hiballs later the grandfather's-banjo-clock announces it is time to trek along. What a chowder party! Good old Charlie pulled out all the stops tonight. Yes sir, nothing but the best, the very best. Charlie's got himself a swell little place there and knows how to go first class.

Charlie displays all the stigmata of success. He drives a big car, belongs to the best country club, patronizes the finest tailor, drinks the "right" brands of liquor, lives in the most exclusive neighborhood, and—well, you've seen his house, full of "beautiful" things and "brilliant" innovations. But don't be too hard on Charlie. He does make an effort, however ludicrous, to *live* in his house among a terrible confusion and contradiction of furnishings. The honk-and-glare of his parties probably reflect an unconscious effort to shield himself from the impact of his home environment. He is a victim of the idea that if you spend enough on plenty of decoration, that's the way to "fix" a house. It is.

Aside from his business, which is making vacuum cleaners, and he's a whiz at that, very few original ideas dwell in Charlie's head. He's a hundred per cent American, a self-made man and proud of it. He's got a plant downtown that's a dream of engineering skill, functionalism, and good looks. Charlie likes to spend a lot of his time at the plant; Mrs. Charlie says too much time. But somehow, and he doesn't quite know why, he feels more at home there.

Charlie feels at home at work because he knows what he is doing; everything around the plant has sense and meaning. The offices are comfortable and good-looking, the workshops are well arranged, and the building is simple and well designed. Why, then, does he live in such a scrambled atmosphere? Does he leave it all up to Mrs. Charlie? Not entirely. They have perpetrated this fraud together.

Suppose one day Charlie opens his eyes and realizes that home should never be like this. He begins to wonder what good taste means. "Does it mean the way that old fossil Elmsworthy lives, all one style, with genuine antiques, in a perfect copy of an old English hall jammed with transplanted atmosphere, uncomfortable, cold, unlivable?" If that's what they call good taste, he doesn't want any part of it. "And who in blazes," Charlie demands, "are *they?*"

They are everybody—designers, decorators, manufacturers, editors, salespeople, customers. Some of them attempt to set the style and make the fashion, and others follow. And what they say and what they mean is made of all sorts of sense and nonsense.

Who does know, then? Who are the arbiters of taste? Designers and decorators, the good ones, are the primary arbiters of taste, and although their approaches differ and their conclusions vary, they are in general agreement. In study and experience they have learned to appraise and accept good things and discard phonies. But there is no definite set of rules evolved out of their experience for us to follow.

We can start, however, by taking a thoughtful look. Whether it's a national monument, castle, house, rabbit hutch, or just a little something to put on the mantelpiece, if it's not good-looking it's not desirable.

Fads, Fashions—Fooey!

The market place is getting bigger all the time, and its food is fashion. Public notice of a new design starts a fad; when public acceptance is enthusiastic it becomes a style, and if it is accepted generally, it becomes fashion. Wonderful and peculiar things derive from this constant necessity for a change. At the time of its inception, acceptance, and use, the current fashion seems good, it may even seem to be "the best thing yet."

A fashionable woman dresses almost entirely in the style of the moment, and when the "new look" sags she renovates her wardrobe. Houses are a different matter; the folly of liquidating the household and its effects every few years is obvious.

One of the most interesting creative sources of styles and fashions is archeological accident. Some curious scientist, care-

. . . a careless peasant stumbles upon a lost civilization . . .

less child, or peasant stumbles upon a lost civilization. If it strikes a responsive chord, we find all sorts of decorative titbits to seize upon. The great unearthing of Pompeii, forgotten all during the Middle Ages, began in 1763, at a time when European esthetes were shooting the works on "Classic Culture." Parks featured Greco-Roman temples of love and fake ruins. Literature, poetry, drama, and

. . . part woman, part Flemish twist . . .

opera swarmed with gods and goddesses of the ancients. Creatures bared to the waist, part woman, part Flemish twist, languished with wings aflutter against the furniture. In all of man's long, bumbling journey from the cave this was thought to be the destination—the epitome of intellectual and artistic achievement.

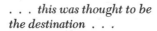

. . . this was thought to be the destination . . .

. . . *Wedgwood* . . .

The Pompeian diggings instituted a total fashion in France and influenced all Europe. In England its immortality was reinsured by the brothers Adam and Josiah Wedgwood. And only a decade or so later the American eagle, just learning to fly, was a bird with a classic background, and the names "Republic" and "Senate" were borrowed from ancient Rome.

In France the little Corsican needed food for his troops and fame for his future, and Italy furnished both. When he returned in triumph, the "Consulate" was established— a term borrowed from Rome—and Napoleon appointed the designers, Percier and Fontaine, who reiterated the classic for posterity. Friezes frozen in the delicate designs of Pompeii decorated walls and ceilings; vases found in tombs were placed in recesses

. . . *Percier and Fontaine reiterated the classic* . . .

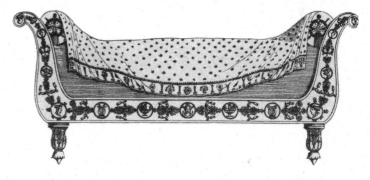

. . . *designs of Pompeii-decorated walls and ceilings* . . .

49

imitating ancient columbaria; panther's muzzle and claw and other insignia of Bacchus rioted everywhere. Chimeras of outlandish aspect were *le dernier cri*. Even Pauline, Bonaparte's beautiful sister, was immortalized in snow-white marble as a reclining Venus.

Napoleon's conquest of Egypt introduced another style to France. The Obélisque Luxor, brought from the Nile, still stands in the Place de la Concorde, but the Egyptian was not much of an influence on the rest of Europe. People were still aping the grandeur that was Rome; they saw no reason to emulate the Pharaohs. Perhaps if Napoleon's Russian campaign had borne fruit, instead of withering in that dreadful winter, Paris would abound with turnip-shaped cupolas and another style might have overshadowed the classic.

We have had this chance in our own time. The discovery of Tutankhamen's tomb made a great stir but failed to institute a great fashion—except in southern California, where it had a brief flurry in hot-dog stands and cinema palaces. If it had won general acceptance, we might have had public buildings like pyramids and banks like the Sphinx; luckily, archeology was not mistaken for art. This confusion does crop up, usually to the detriment of good taste.

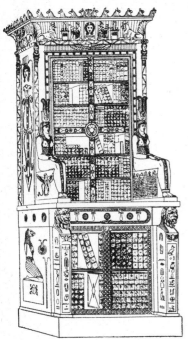

. . . Egypt introduced another style to France . . .

There is a reverse example: recently an archeological collection in one of our largest universities was "rediscovered" and moved to the art department. It was

. . . "Egyptian" hot-dog stand . . .

found to include primitive works from the South Seas, Africa, and the Americas that are valued today for their naïve, uninhibited design. They now serve as artistic examples of native art rather than aboriginal curiosities.

In 1893, at the Chicago Exposition, a group of eminent artists and architects sat at a council table and once again it was decreed that the best of all possible worlds was that of ancient Greece and Rome. They predicted that their re-creation of the "Classic" for the Exposition would seize the imagination of the country and become the fashion. Sullivan, America's first great modern architect, whose own building was the most original contribution, saw the plan for the fraud it was and foresaw that the damage done by the fair would last for half a century. Nor was he wrong.

The panel of experts did not consider that the classic style was singularly out of place in the United States. Our own colonial architecture of New England and the Deep South was an honest interpretation and evolution of the classic from England and, before that, from Italy. Through the years and changes of locale it was adapted and readapted to suit our needs. It had become relatively indigenous and there were many valid reasons for using it. But the panorama of ancient Greco-Roman architecture that sprang up at the World's Columbian Exposition was as foreign to our thoughts and way of life as the Egyptian style had been in the Europe of Napoleon's time. This did not seem to matter. The arbiters of taste had spoken and acted.

The classic blight caused by the Exposition choked inspiration and progress, delayed the development of American architecture and improvements in many fields of design. The architect's skill came to consist of reduplication in every detail of

51

buildings made some two thousand years ago. This grand "detour de force" brought forth the "First National Bank" school of design. For four decades nearly every public building showed the stigma. Schools, stock exchanges, city halls, libraries, post offices, *et al.,* took on the guise of Parthenons, Pantheons, Temples to the Vestal Virgins, Jupiter, Castor and Pollux. Washington, D.C., was done in the classic style.

If the private client contemplating a business structure or mansion couldn't find anything quite to his liking in the existing designs, a variation could be trumped up that was bound to suit. "Pure" copies gave way to wildly adulterated combinations. Many of the interiors were classic or some variation thereof. Sarcophagi and burial urns, laughable pieces and mountebanks in the way of furniture, completed the ridiculous décor. By the time this charade was given the hook, everyone was so fed up with any reminder of this period that even today we prefer to forget one of its saving graces. The authentic sculptures sometimes used were often first-class works of art. Now dealers and collectors will buy Gandhara heads from North India which show the Hellenistic influence of Alexander's conquest and ignore the original inspiration from Greece. We have made this mistake many times. In discarding a whole style or fashion we often lose its most valuable contribution. For excellence of coloring, composition, use of line and mass, Japanese prints—particularly those by the masters—are as great today as when Whistler first opened our Western eyes to their beauty. Their esthetic value has not lessened because they are not in vogue.

Metropolitan Museum of Art

. . . *Gandhara head* . . .

. . . *original inspiration from Greece* . . .

Metropolitan Museum of Art

52

Not everybody could go the classic. For the next thirty years or so there were irruptions of French châteaux, Tudor and Stuart manor houses, Italian *palazzi,* villas of Riviera and Hispano-Moresque types. Few were pure examples, contorted as they were to the whim of architect and client. But by the general public, to whom they were hitherto unknown, they were thought to be proper. Made of alien or unsuitable materials, these styles too were opposed to our times, temperaments, climates, lives, and heritages. Their bastardization made matters worse.

. . . *"fine" things in*
"the right style" . . .

The next fatal step, after acquiring the pseudo-Elizabethan shooting box or what-have-you, was to cram it with "fine" things in "the right style." There weren't many who could afford authentic pieces, and few knew the difference anyway. So the European and American workshops and factories turned out copies of all kinds by the boatload and carload. Baronial halls and Venetian palaces built on the sites of Indian massacres and alligator swamps were cluttered with pompous frauds. Porcelain caryatids staggered under various burdens; rugs and carpets had unpronounceable, exotic names; ecclesiastic vestments and statues of martyred saints stood uncomfortably close to sedan chairs serving as telephone booths. From Jacobean cupboards issued the voices of Amos and Andy, and Italianate jewel coffers contained Havana panetellas.

Some fads are created for a fast turnover, taken up with wild enthusiasm, done to death, and sink into oblivion. But fashions, more constant in their times, often have recurring cycles of popularity, reminding us that we cannot escape or evade the past. Some fashions of years gone by serve us well, but others are out of place and step today.

. . . Gothic, Rococo, and Chinese interwoven by Chippendale . . .

The Gothic, Rococo, and Chinese styles interwoven by Chippendale must have been upsetting notes in the décor even in their time. The eye jumps nervously from one ornament to another, finding no rest or reason; even as remedies for boredom, the cure is worse than the disease. The so-called esthetic theory

let design
like nature! . . .

behind the creation of the Rococo, "Let design grow like nature!" was used later as a peg on which to hang another style. *Art Nouveau,* the design motif of the Paris exposition in 1900, eclipsed its predecessor *Neo-Grec.* Neo-Grec was a style little noticed outside of its birthplace and had as much in common with the land of the Acropolis as a fry cook has with Plato. Art Nouveau's characteristic design was reflected not only in furniture, china, glass, and most household appurte-

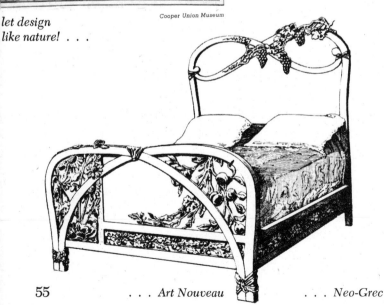

55   . . . *Art Nouveau*   . . . *Neo-Grec*

nances, but was used widely in architecture, typography, and layouts, and in the fine arts. The decorative touches of the Paris subway, built to solve the traffic problem of the celebration, also echoed the motifs of Art Nouveau. Today we look upon Chippendale's caprices as eccentric, perhaps not in style; but the name Chippendale has never gone out of fashion. Hundreds of his designs are less original, more unsuitable than many from the all-but-forgotten period of Art Nouveau.

The "Antique" craze was the scream in the 1920s. It wasn't "smart" to have anything that looked new. Fabrics were produced in pale, time-faded shades; "antique satin," a material with a peculiar worn look, was a best seller. If furniture wasn't authentically "period," the dealers would boast that the finish applied to it was an exact copy of the patina of age. Painted surfaces were crackled to make a hot-off-the-production-line piece look as if it had weathered many a bleak winter and scorching summer. Or off-white, sometimes called oyster white, was painted on, barnyard brown was smeared on top of that, a little rubbed off, and *voilà*, an antique accent! Honest polished brass, copper, or bronze became difficult to sell, so it was finished at the factory in tarnished effects. Ironwork, used on the exterior and interior of houses, had to give the impression that it, too, had withstood many a season's inclement blasts. A chap in Italy made a great success supplying this demand. Wrought iron was taken from his workshop and bathed in a Venetian canal for six months, where it aged prematurely and was exactly what those crazy Americans wanted.

The European manufacturers of antiques contrived astounding ways of fabricating fakes. The doubtful dealers presented them to their American clients as "fine old pieces of the period" —whatever that might be. Even a collector with a sharp eye was frequently fooled by the expertness of the forgeries. One system of manufacture, almost impossible of detection, was to make furniture with the same tools, in the same way, of the same materials as the authentic pieces had been made. When the article was finished, a corps of small boys was employed to rub their hands over it—and if they had forgotten to wash them, so much the better. After an extended period of massage, it looked as if it had been kicking around for some time. Often, in order to hoodwink those who considered themselves clever, the makers of fakes would carry the process a couple of steps farther. They would take a finished piece and push it out of a second-story window or down a wide flight of stone stairs. The chips could fall where they might. They were gathered up and the piece rebuilt. The dealer, presenting it in his showroom, would protest that, being an honest man, he could not let you think it was in mint condition; a perfect piece of the period would, of course, be worth much more. He would point out the splendid "restoration," so cleverly done as to be nearly unnoticeable. Any remaining doubts were exorcised, and the sale was made.

. . . they would push it out a second-story window . . .

The antique craze is by no means strictly modern. The ancient Romans collected antique Greek sculpture, and when the authentic pieces were exhausted, artful copies were made and undoubtedly sold as "genuine Athenian." For Hellas was the old world of the Latin new world, and it was a sign of culture and intellect to emulate it.

Preoccupation with antique art and design, to the exclusion of new expressions, casts an angry gloom over those who are creating the current style. Early in the eighteenth century Hogarth complained that the modern English painter found it hard to compete with "dead relics of the past." The picture dealers were then making a great fuss over the Italian painters of a century or so before, and local talent was being more or less ignored.

In the 1930s the revival of the Victorian style fouled up the scene. When the antique dealers had combed the market to baldness for the popular European and indigenous styles, trade needed the needle and the "Victorian" was it. The secondhand dealers arranged a generous supply and fixed it so customers could "discover" a quaint piece for a bargain price. Guests were impaled on clots of fruit carved on chairs and settees, or to-bogganed off the slick horsehair upholstery. Sometimes the furniture was recovered in chintzes and other fabrics; it was bleached, pickled, painted, and gilded. If one were lucky enough to own a rosewood piece from the 1850s, it was a superior example. But most people didn't discriminate; they were collecting "heirlooms."

. . . guests were impaled on clots of fruit . . .

Style is set not only by the arbiters of fashion and the mandates of the famous; methods and materials dictate the birth of scores of new things.

The development of a new material or a novel use for an old one or a new method of manufacture is a challenge that invariably yields a host of innovations. Technological progress creates the latest thing but doesn't always bring us nearer economy, practicality, or a good effect.

For madness in method, the "rustication" of 1600 to 1750 is an example. Stone, straight and smooth from the quarry, was attacked by hammer and chisel in an attempt to make it resemble a natural freak. These shaggy members were incorporated in the façade of buildings. The result was a pox as bad

. . . *"rustication"* . . .

as a *jazz-finish* wall on a stucco cottage. The black patina of a century of London fog or ten years of Los Angeles smog can do nothing to translate this curse into a blessing.

The skyscraper, that American phenomenon whose development was possible only because of the use of structural steel, masqueraded in several imported styles. Instead of using the new material to fit its properties, the terra cotta that veneered it was pressed and molded and messed up. Cornices, columns, flying buttresses, and arches, suitable and necessary if built in stone, meaninglessly appeared in the new type of structure, to whose use in function and form it was superfluous.

Cantilevered construction and off-angle walls tend toward a forced note today. When they are necessary to solve an architectural problem, honesty is added to style, but these clichés may become so tiresome that we will discard them in a few years.

Like the parent of a precocious child, it's a temptation to see what a precocious machine can be made to do. The perfection of the sawing machine made designers, builders, and carpenters delirious. The wild band-saw work of the seventies and eighties, dripping from the eaves of houses all over the nation, became the rage.

American know-how made fancywork in pressed glass possible. Tinkering with this process began early in the nineteenth century. The Sandwich and Boston Glass Company made many

59

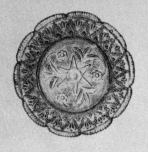

. . . *Sandwich Glass* . . .

familiar examples; they are popular collector's items today. As records of intricate designs fashioned by an old machine method, they are interesting, though esthetically unappealing, and the many copies on the market seem pointless jokes.

Besides forgetting good design, when overcome by the adaptability of certain materials, we often overlook the demands of economy and practicality. It is a common delusion that solid wood is better than veneer, marble superior to terrazzo, silk finer than nylon. A salesman may boast that a desk is solid mahogany, but in many phases of construction, modern laminated plywood is stronger than solid wood, lighter, and more serviceable, being nearly impervious to temperature intensities and changes. Terrazzo, which is ground-up marble combined with cement, is used for floors and even murals and table tops. It serves the same purposes as solid marble but with many more desirable qualities—several colors can be used, making a muted new color, or other materials can be imbedded in it with great scope of design.

Discovery of new mate-

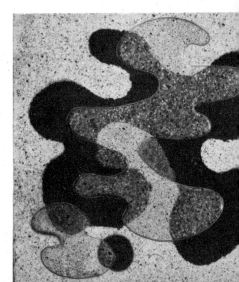

. . . *excellent use of terrazzo by Margaret Bruton* . . .

rials is challenging and stimulating, but sometimes, in the excitement of exploiting them, their properties obscure intelligent design and good use. Before the unexpected denouement at Hiroshima, ours was called the "Plastics Age." These new materials, whose forms and uses we have hardly begun to discover, are replacing thousands less efficient.

At first the plain, flat, transparent sheets of plastic which could be bent, cut, and laminated were put to all sorts of unsuitable uses. Ridiculous doodles in design for cigarette boxes, book ends, wastebaskets, lamps, and light fixtures appeared on the market. Now that the first abandoned experimenting with the structural possibilities of the material is over, more common-sense use is being made of it.

The familiar plastic used for shower curtains has not been exploited enough. We think of it as practical and serviceable, little more. But divorced from associations, it is pleasing to look at and could be used, in one of its attractive colors, to block an ugly view, to diffuse light in a bedroom or studio living room. Upholstery plastic has not been entirely accepted in the fashionable world. It has been introduced for hard usage, the ravages of children, rumpus rooms—in which any disaster might happen—for utility rooms and public places. It has been mottled and grained to look like leather, in the snobbish notion that if it is mistaken for something else its social standing will improve. The only time it gives a bad impression is when it's made to look like something else. As itself —plain, slick, handsome, in generous widths, unlimited lengths, in a variety of exciting colors, nearly indestructible—it is something new and different in the best sense.

. . . *plastic grained to look like leather* . . .

Another of science's recent contributions is nylon. Perhaps because it was initially rather high in price and was used to make attractive things in women's fashions, there is not much snob resistance to it. There are a few house-proud people who are convinced that the tenuous thread of the worm is the *ne plus ultra* of fashion and nylon only a crass substitute, and that if you can have "the real thing" why settle for anything less. They're still thinking the way Grandma did when she shot the works and put silk covers on the parlor suite. Grandpa and the little ones were barred except on formal occasions when the room was exhibited to bolster Grandma's feeling of social superiority. No doubt some of her friends were envious. It was something to be in style, but everything to be in the most expensive style.

We are prone to forget that a material of quality can be made with different ingredients and in many ways. Lyons silk stands for top quality; it has a more famous name in the world than hand-woven Italian silk, although it is made on the machine loom. We are used to the finest silk made by mechanical means and accept it unquestioningly. As nylon becomes more adapted to the uses for which it is uniquely fitted, it will replace many other fabrics. Nylon is not an imitation of any other material but has valuable synthetic qualities lacking in the natural fabrics; it can substitute in weave and effect for nearly all of them.

Imitation, the use of one material or method to look like another, is a popular whimsey. Some years ago wall hangings and tapestries were "in"; very few were easy on the eyes. The market was flooded with them; many were crude imitations painted on a rep cloth to give the impression of a tapestry weave. We would rock with laughter if we caught sight of one today. But not long ago we were furnished with a curious twist of the same idea and no one cracked a smile. A collection of Gobelin tapestries designed by illustrious French modern artists toured our museums. They were such meticulous copies of the artists' paintings that the minutest brush strokes had been painstakingly reproduced; it was hard from a slight distance to tell what they were. "Aren't they amazing!" the onlookers said, pleased and thunderstruck. "They look just like paintings." Paintings to look like tapestries—tapestries to look like paintings!

Masterful craftsmanship in a new material sets many long-lasting styles. The perfection of hard-paste porcelain in eighteenth-century Europe gave the artisans of that time a flexible material amenable to complex designs and abandoned colorful decoration—a fashionable luxury when first made, it is still in style. There are thousands of collectors of antique examples. Many of the most sought-after are worthless from the point of view of beauty. Collections in museums, antique shops, and in private hands show what scarecrows can be born of fine craft and bad design. Figure groups in twisted, awkward poses with expressions indistinguishable from their bovine or ovine companions; malformed children, their black-dotted eyes sliding off their cheekbones; lovers in coy and painful postures—all "authentic" and eminently resalable; ungainly vases, pots, and jars alight with angry colors—all "correctly marked" and highly valued. There is nothing wrong with the material: it is high-fired and strong; it takes a fine glaze; models can be reduplicated, making it generally available. And when the designs are in the hands of artists rather than pot bakers it is worthy of its continued popularity.

Some new things that excite general notice are hardly re-

. . . Britannia metal, responsible for these abominations . . .

Cooper Union Museum Library

64

membered a decade later. Britannia metal, an alloy of antimony, was combined with electroplating, making possible the casting of involved shapes at minimum cost. The process was responsible for some of the prominent abominations of the early nineteenth century. Though britannia metal is still manufactured, newer economical methods and uses for other metals have relegated it to a minor place. Today it appears on the market in several good designs.

Among the strange parents of fads and styles is the patriotic gesture or sensational occurrence. One of the most amusing procreators was Montgolfier's successful balloon levitation over Paris in 1783. The designers' resultant flights of fancy in commemoration of this event took the form of chairs whose backs were shaped like the famous gasbag, chandeliers, clocks, and fabric patterns duplicating the balloon. If Lindbergh's flight had taken place in an age when there were fewer distractions, *The Spirit of Saint Louis* would no doubt have served as inspiration for a tremendous style. But the amazing twenties were rushing by and there were too many other startling things happening to take time to re-create the epic trip in design and ornament.

Novelty is a necessary and pleasant part of life. It tickles the imagination and propels progress. But as we trace some of the causes of style and fashion—whim, accident, audacity—we see how erratic the results may be. It is not likely that through them we can discover good taste.

Nostalgically Yours

I'm just looking around . . .

"I'm just looking around," "I don't really know what I want," "I know exactly what I want," "I don't know what's good but I do know what I like," customers will say. They may be telling the bald truth or kidding themselves. They may not be as definite or dilatory as they would have you believe; they may be like a beagle on the scent of a fox, proudly ignorant but positive, or knowledgeable but perplexed.

We all have our own ideas of what makes a desirable background for living. Our personal taste is often based on pleasant or unpleasant reactions, and because we seldom are aware of the reasons that cause the reactions we have little control over them.

. . . I don't really know what I want . . .

. . . I don't know what's good but I do know what I like . . .

What makes Joan wince at a green vase and her sister Mary choose it in preference to all others? Does the color remind Joan unconsciously of the wall paper in the room where she was so miserable with the measles? The time that nasty Airedale knocked her down on the wet lawn and ruined her party dress? Maybe it's something entirely different, but there's probably some unpleasant association somewhere in the past. And what makes Mary buy the vase? Does the color remind her of the curtains in her old room where she was always comfy? Or the tie that dear Floyd had on when he finally proposed? Perhaps it's neither of these things, but a pleasant association is probably behind her preference.

Suppose we get acquainted with these two sisters. They grew up together in a comfortable old house. Mary married as soon as she graduated from college, and she and her husband moved into a new housing development in their home town. They like living in the sticks and Floyd doesn't mind commuting. The real-estate agent said the house was the latest thing in building, "a kinda modern farmhouse style." But it isn't really extreme. It has "a normal, two-way pitch roof," not one of those "ugly shed roofs" that Mary can't stand. It has "a decent floor plan," not one of "those awful arrangements they're using now with no feeling of privacy, seclusion, or protection, what they call an open, circulating plan, where cooking odors and noise freely circulate because there are only curtains or inadequate partitions between the sleeping, living, eating, cooking areas; with great walls of floor-to-ceiling glass making you feel completely exposed to the elements, nature, and the neighbors; with almost no way of shutting out the light even if curtains are drawn across the mammoth windows." In such a house Mary would have no repose, comfort, security, or happiness. She would feel like a bird in a bottle.

Mary's house has a living room that is cheerful and cozy, and a separate dining room where she can set a party table without being gaped at and which she can shut off after dinner, leaving the cleaning up until everyone's gone home. The bedroom is small but in the quietest corner of the house, and when Floyd has the boys over for poker Mary doesn't hear them. The windows in the house are divided into small panes that break the monotony of the street and garden views and are so placed that shelves, bookcases, and other furniture arrangements can go beneath them.

Joan got a job when she finished college and soon graduated into a "position," but Stu came along and she gave it all up to become a housewife. Joan and her husband found an apartment in the metropolis where work and entertainment are conveniently near. The real-estate agent said the apartment was "the best kind of modern, as contemporary as tomorrow." Joan, who was unconsciously oppressed by the feeling of being confined in the house of her childhood, by heavily foliaged trees and many little rooms with small-paned windows, is perfectly happy in her new environment. The apartment on the top floor with a fine view is bright, light, and airy. There are only three rooms, but they look larger than they really are because they have several sections of floor-to-ceiling windows that "give a wonderful feeling of being unconfined and free." Joan thinks it's heaven to be awakened by the sun streaming in through the gauzy bedroom curtains.

When Mary settled for better or worse the family gave her a choice of some of the "nice old things" that had been around as long as she could remember. She took those that had always appealed to her most and picked up a few others elsewhere that she particularly liked. She made her own ruffled curtains and tiebacks in simple patterns. The kitchen was given a homey air by painting it a warm yellow and using touches of bright red in the dining alcove on the cushions of the captain's chairs and on scalloped curtains and table mats. Mary is a gifted and enthusiastic cook. Floyd says, "There's no monkey business about her food." Mary has a weakness for ornaments. If one clutches at her fancy and she can afford it, she'll buy it without thinking where it might be used or if it is suitable for a certain room. The house is a hodgepodge of many styles and periods. It mirrors Mary's domesticity and has Floyd's imprint on it too. He makes models of small boats, and the best examples have been arranged on one wall above the shelves that hold his modest collection of sailing trophies. The house, particularly the bedroom, is more feminine looking than masculine. But Mary's husband doesn't care. Shucks, he's got a comfortable, happy home. He doesn't "know anything about fixing a house. Why shouldn't she have it the way she wants it?"

Joan and Stu collaborated on the choice of furnishings for their apartment. They firmly declined offers of "nice old family pieces." They wanted "efficient, attractive, strictly modern things" and "no clutter." They read a lot of magazines and decided on a "controlled color scheme of smart, muted shades, plain carpets, blond furniture, and a few touches of good, decorative accessories chosen with care for the right spot." The curtains, slip covers, and bedspread, made by the store where they bought most of their furnishings, are all strictly tailored, with interesting textures and soft colors but "*no* busy design!" The kitchen, white and neat, is only for cooking, and the end of the living room serves for dining. Joan likes to give "smart little dinners with sophisticated food"—casserole dishes simmered in wine, plain green salads, fruit and cheeses for dessert, or, on gala occasions, crêpes Suzette served from a chafing dish at the table. It is obvious that the apartment is the result of a studied plan; everything "harmonizes" and there are no superfluous or jarring notes. It is an excellent example of the kind of nest for newlyweds that the magazines feature so extensively and which served Joan and Stu as the inspiration for putting it together. It's a background neither masculine nor feminine; even the bedroom, with its large chests, plain lamps, tailored look, and lack of extracurricular adornment, is strictly neuter.

When Mary married she received a conglomeration of wedding presents. There were a few attic candidates among them, but most have been put to some kind of use. When Joan embraced wedded bliss she fared better. Everyone knew that "Joan has very good taste and only likes modern." Relatives and friends were asked to consult listings of the patterns she selected for china, silver, glassware, and linens at the smart store in town which features this service. The system works well all around. The bride is supplied with her choice of the niceties of housekeeping, and the store avoids ruptured tempers and hurt feelings which often occur when presents are returned. Of course the lamp from Aunt Sarah was a disaster—dolphins on tiptail, relic from a turn-of-the-century trip to Venice. Aunt Sarah thinks it's beautiful, not because it has any claim to good looks but because it is associated in her mind with her happy honeymoon beside the Adriatic.

Mary's china set has roses on it. When she chose it she didn't know that of all the designs on china, roses are the favorite. Their popularity can be traced to their association with romance and the fact that roses grow nearly everywhere and can be immediately identified in a design—everyone knows what they are. Joan is "sick of the sight of roses" or "any of the other hackneyed china designs." She would choose any other subject, stylized in design, and preferably none at all. She has an oatmeal-colored pottery set for every day and plain white china in coupe shapes for more formal occasions.

Until she can buy some "really fine pictures by a recognized contemporary artist," Joan has hung a Van Gogh and a Gauguin print. She discarded the idea of paying a few dollars more for a couple of water colors by an "unknown modern." She thought it better to be "sure of having something good even if it was a reproduction." But Mary has quite a few original paintings scattered about her house. She found most of them in second-hand shops and bought them because the subjects—animals, flowers, and snow scenes—appealed to her. She hasn't gotten around to deciphering the artists' signatures.

Joan's apartment strikes Mary as being a little "impersonal," a bit severe, and rather cold; secretly she thinks it's not at all homey or cozy. She knows Joan is "the one with taste" and that her apartment is certainly "smart and stylish." She feels she's probably wrong in not thinking it is perfect. Mary's house would drive Joan crazy. "Nothing matches, nothing goes together, everything's a little helter-skelter, and all those dust catchers!" Privately, she thinks it's a mess.

What causes these divergent tastes? Both Mary and Joan bloomed on the same tree in the same atmosphere. Is Mary the family norm and Joan the freak of a shuffle in chromosomes? Does Mary's security depend on being sheltered and confined in familiar surroundings with well-known and loved associations? Is Joan's impulse to rebel against familiar surroundings a sign that they weren't well loved by her and don't spell security? Is she more normal in wanting a change, in striking out to make her own way of life, in surrounding herself with the taste of her own generation? Is Mary's taste non-progressive, corny, dull? Is Joan's progressive, smart, stimulating?

If psychiatrists knew more about decoration or decorators more of psychiatry, it should be possible to make a telling analysis by studying the house without ever seeing the tenants. Not only their temperaments and physical characteristics but their inner desires and fears could be pictured within the frame of their surroundings.

When Joan goes into a store and says, "I know exactly what I want," does she really know? When Mary wanders in and says, "I'm just looking around. I don't know what I want," is she so unsure? Joan may make a purchase and have it wrapped while Mary is still musing over the first display inside the front door. But from the other side of the counter, things are not always as they seem, and until psychoanalysis invades store-keeping, the salesman can make his own diagnosis with a fair percentage of hits.

There is a better than even chance that Mary is free and unconventional and Joan an enslaved and limited conformist. Mary may be chuck-full of reminders, unconscious reactions, and associations which manifest themselves in the things with which she chooses to live. But she is reacting normally. And she is reacting above normal with the attitude that although she likes certain things, she doesn't expect you to like them. She doesn't say they're good taste, but *her* taste. She may like a house that gives her a feeling of being protected, sheltered, cuddled, but so do a lot of other people. The house looks like Mary's and Floyd's house, not like a picture in a magazine—

there is too much variety, too little scheme or plan for that. But there is originality there too, in the combination of things not made to go together but that somehow look well together, and there is interest in the many personal things, the hobbies and caprices that ornament it. Mary's house is more work than Joan's decoratively economical apartment, but Mary finds so much pleasure in all the things she's collected under her roof, she does it cheerfully. Mary would be surprised to learn that she usually knows exactly what she wants when she sees it among a wide selection of things in a store. And in expressing *herself* she is individual and progressive. She is more conscious of new recipes and ingenious household gadgets shown in the magazines than decorating copy, although she absorbs more of this than she realizes and rejects most of it. She is not a disciple of "the latest thing," she is not easily influenced, and she and those like her are not a good market for advertising campaigns with snob appeal. She does not care what the Joneses are doing unless she knows and likes them.

Joan may think she has cut loose from the past by refusing to have anything around remindful of it. She may be more a child of the mid-twentieth century than Mary by choosing to live in plain, light, generously glassed rooms. She may like only the modern things considered "smart" and "in perfect taste." She too is reacting normally; many people feel the same way. And she is reacting normally with the attitude that this is the best way to live and if you have "any taste" you'll choose to live this way. Her home looks like a great many young couples' homes, like a picture in a magazine illustrating an article on how to furnish a small apartment. There is little variety but the scheme has been well planned and successfully worked out. There is no originality but everything goes together and looks well together, and nothing is in evidence that points to a hobby of the master or mistress unless we consider the record collection embracing a selection of long-hairs from Debussy to the present day, some hot jazz, and a Book-of-the-Month Club library. But there are no memorabilia, and caprice is a stranger here. Joan is quick to pick up suggestions from other people's smart, modern places and the profuse decorating copy and illustrations in the magazines. She has a good critical sense and chooses the suitable suggestion or idea for her purpose. Joan wouldn't believe that she really doesn't know what she wants in the varied selection of a store. She buys the "name," and unless she finds something which, through advertising or display, she recognizes as being "good," she will not consider it. Without a familiar label, she has difficulty recognizing a superior product.

In her own new home she is a disciple of "the latest thing," she is easily influenced. She and those like her are the market for advertising campaigns with snob appeal. Joan is not sure of what she likes but only what she is told it's "smart" to like and what she believes she *should* like. Someday she may find that she has developed a personal taste which will help her add interest to her home and keep it from being just anybody's fashionable apartment. But in the meantime she is much concerned with what the Joneses are doing. She doesn't know them and perhaps wouldn't like them, but "the Joneses are the smartest young couple in town."

How dear to our hearts are the things we remember happily. The butter-and-egg man who has gained a well-earned retirement after a lifetime of hectic competition yearns for the Dresden lamp. And with reason. It lights up for him an almost forgotten time in his youth. Filet mignon sold for twenty-five

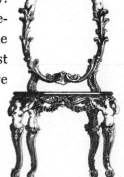

75

. . . how dear to our hearts are the things we remember happily . . .

*. . . he yearns for
the Dresden lamp . . .*

cents a pound. Pa had a steady little business, took two hours off at noon, walked home for a five-course "dinner," and had time for a nap afterward. You sparked your girl at the Sunday concerts in the park, a visit to the next town was the big excitement and took all day by horse and buggy, whisky was ten cents a shot, and the free lunch at the bar was loaded with substantial vittles.

Besides our own peculiar preferences, there are many basic desires shared by all of us that influence our habits and habitats. If we can put aside a little extra we often spend it under our own roofs. The desire for comfort is the goal of everyone. It is the nature of woman in our society to be preoccupied with personal adornment and an enticing setting for her charms. It is custom for the male to recognize that his importance is largely judged by the way he lives. We all have the gregarious instinct, and when we conduct a roundup of the herd we're gratified to hear noises of appreciation making the rafters resound.

Just as there are preferences and prejudices that grow out of personal experience and common basic desires, there are mass reactions based on socio-emotional reasons. We turn against many things that nudge our subconscious on the unhappy side. Some modern furniture made of chrome-plated metal is unpleasantly associated in a good many minds with doctors' and dentists' offices. Although much of it is

Knoll Associates, Inc.

. . . well designed for utility . . .

well designed and suitable for home use, it is either rejected entirely or suffered purely for utility in the kitchen and dining nook. Even some of the more luxurious modern furniture is refused on the premise that a roomful of it creates the impersonal, commercial atmosphere of a hotel, airline office, or executive's sanctum. White, sterile-looking kitchens affect many people adversely. They seem designed for clinical rather than gastronomical explorations. They represent a reminder of the painful necessities instead of the pleasant niceties of life.

But there are as many who embrace the expressions of the ultramodern without reservation. These "progressives" are not interested in the family tree or the "traditional" kind of house or furnishings. They are the great market for today's and tomorrow's art and design. "Modern" signifies progress and all the good things it brings. More people, as American generations add up, are getting farther away from a tie with "the old country." The land from which our forefathers emigrated becomes increasingly a symbol of an unstable society that has forced us into international complications and disasters from which we would like to escape. The "traditional" house and furnishings have indirectly taken on the stigma of these unpleasant associations. As this feeling grows, Americans in greater numbers turn to modern interpretations as symbols of a happy security.

The lords of the great English manor houses in the late sixteenth and early seventeenth centuries were playing the same tune backward. They felt a certain cultural weakness in their own rugged society and so imported Italian artisans to add decorative unfamiliarities to their familiar haunts. Mass

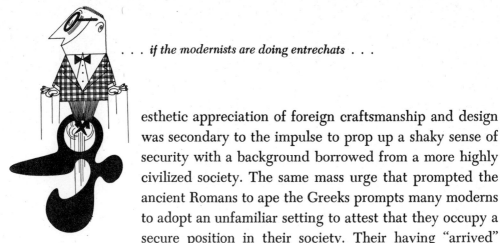

esthetic appreciation of foreign craftsmanship and design was secondary to the impulse to prop up a shaky sense of security with a background borrowed from a more highly civilized society. The same mass urge that prompted the ancient Romans to ape the Greeks prompts many moderns to adopt an unfamiliar setting to attest that they occupy a secure position in their society. Their having "arrived" may be heralded by a house in traditional or contemporary style, or they may belong to the small coterie of the *avant-garde* who regard any traditional and most contemporary settings as "unbearably trite," "banal." The avant-garde try not to be seen with anything at all "derivative." They are interested in the most obscure art forms. If the modern enthusiasts are doing entrechats over the work of Henry Moore, they might turn away from him to the sculpture of an eighty-year-old Maori living in a Philadelphia basement. Art Tatum might be considered "too obvious," but a stranger who tickles the keys only for private pressings could create a sensation. They usually favor absolute severity in decoration and non-conformist types of décor, unremindful of the past and with as little recognition of the present as possible, and would use apple boxes rather than a popular good-looking bookcase. They often promote the early work of modern designers but abandon them when they've "made good with the crowd," even though their later work may be superior. There are genuine intellectuals in this group but there are more phonies. Their common psychological need is to be in a class by themselves. The group's well-informed members are no doubt seeking "basic answers," while the fakers hide their lack of knowledge by an addiction to things without precedent for which they can't be criticized on any familiar basis.

Basic psychological drives change the cultures and styles of societies and often add a touch of comic relief. In the Victorian or, more aptly, the early Grover Cleveland period, Turkish Corners were the thing. In a décor of prim discomfort cluttered up with masses of meaningless decorative objects, this exotic phenomenon stood out like a cooch dancer at a church social. Above the low couch, tumorous with pillows, was a canopy upheld by imitation spears. The couch and fragmentary tent were draped with oriental rugs or materials presumed to give an "Eastern" effect. The usual unsubstantial table beside this Levantine lair held a water pipe or other tourist trinket from the bazaars. Was this pseudo-voluptuary's couch the manifestation of a hidden desire to cast off the strictures of the period—when proper behavior forbade a lady to expose the buttons on her ill-fitting shoe?

. . . Turkish corners were the thing . . .

The present popularity of primitive sculptures among esthetes may have a psychological persuasion. Paradoxically, many of the people who shun the reminders of "the old country" and go all out for "modern" are devotees of the primitive cult. These wood carvings are consciously appreciated for their crude, direct design, but no doubt they are also symbols of an aboriginal society which, to our minds, is a simple, uninhibited way of life far removed from the blocks and repressions of our fast-paced, complex Western civilization. The modern con-

79

noisseur who collects this type of primitive art and the chap who pins up a calendar with a hula girl on it are both expressing their own interpretation of the basic urge to "get away from it all."

We admire and desire the things that are symbols of security or represent what we imagine will make our lives easy and pleasant. Let us by all means arrange to have more of them around us. The ego needs an occasional builder-upper, a psychic vitamin now and then. But most often, when we say something is beautiful or terrible, we mean that *we* like or dislike it; it makes us purr and sometimes forget that it may not be catnip to the general. Our reactions, based on unique personal experiences, influence our choices but can't be depended upon to guide us to good looks or good taste.

The Joneses Are Jerks

"Live your own life!" This is a credo widely recommended in advertising, articles, and best sellers. "Be yourself!" strikes some as an admonition impossible of realization, others as an inescapable chore, and a few as an outright insult. The idea of living your own life, being yourself, is both simple and involved and will go on being a basic and complex preoccupation as long as there's anything stirring in our upper stories, or lower for that matter.

Spiritually, "living your own life" and "being yourself" are unique problems for everyone, with a different answer for each. Materially, the problem isn't as unique and the answers are more uniform. On the subject of the houses we live in and the furnishings we live with, why not say everyone is being himself and let it go at that? In the second half of the twentieth century, a realistic age, people are constantly simplifying their

83

lives—or trying to. A set pattern is rarer; building and decorating are more elastic.

Certainly many of us are living the way we choose to live —or at least having a whirl at it. But some of us are leading a different kind of life or living in a different environment than we did a few years ago. Others are stuck with a way of living that seemed all right at the time they fashioned it or when it was imposed upon them. After a time, however, they are jolted into the discovery that it is somehow all wrong. Others are making the mistake of choosing an environment which will prove to be unsuitable and awkward.

Even with television, people spend more time away from home than they used to. Henry Ford, motion pictures, labor-saving devices, women in the world of business, more schools and day nurseries, the dissemination of entertainment and cultural pursuits—lectures, book clubs, and what not—over wider geographical areas have all conspired to get us out of the house. Some of them, goodness knows, we should get out of! The modern woman, who copes with a small family in a compact, easily cared for place, wonders how Grandma managed a big family in a rambling, many-floored house without blowing her top. Grandma often had at least one helper, but even if she didn't, her life in many ways was easier than Granddaughter's is. Except on rare occasions, she stayed home; there were few outside distrac-

. . . Grandma's house . . .

tions; she had plenty of work, but she could take her time about it. There was no feeling of pressure. The family gathered every evening for supper, which was a leisurely affair; no one was rushing to get through, no one was going anywhere. The evening was spent quietly—studying, reading, sewing, talking, or at games. No summons from a telephone, no sound of a radio or phonograph, no TV hypnosis. The rest of the world seemed very remote. Every day's pattern was much the same. The summer might bring a trip to the mountains or seashore, but life was nearly as regulated and quiet in the vacation environment. Home was the place where you got not only shelter and sustenance but whatever entertainment came your way. It was reasonable that the houses were large, often with more than one living room—the usual family gathering place and the rarely used parlor. The house was all things to all members of the family. Friends were usually entertained at home, so it was the custom to set an elaborate table, for dining was a ceremony and a source of entertainment. Grandma's house, in Modern Gothic, cluttered with gewgaws and knickknacks, certainly from our point of view not in the best of taste, seemed excellent to her. The busyness of the decoration probably amused the eye rather than confused it—life was much more simple, the pace was slow, the jitters were then unknown.

Oh yeh? With only the "good" things remembered, that is how many people see Grandma's day. But really we know better. Grandma stayed home because she had to; she was absorbed in the interminable job of keeping house. There was nowhere else to go, and when

. . . *Modern Gothic—1876* . . .

there was, it was hard to get there. Even if she had a hired girl, Grandma superintended the work and very likely lent a hand. She herself usually attended to baking mountains of breads, pies, and cakes, and cooking special dishes that were the family's favorites—all on a balky hand-stoked range which would appall Granddaughter.

Grandma's was a hard life compared to Granddaughter's and the salient reason why Granddaughter, say the experts, out-lives her by a decade or more. Folks didn't have much patience with "nervy females," and when Grandma had the jitters—as she certainly did—she tried to soothe them with cream o' tartar or calomel. On the whole, Grandma had so many tasks and responsibilities that she didn't have the time or inclination to be concerned with good taste in her home. She had plenty of excuse for relying upon the ready-made taste of her time.

But we have no such excuse. We have the leisure, means, and sources to make home comfortable and good-looking. We are all at the mercy of an unplanned universe, ill-designed and chaotic. Only at home have we the privilege of maintaining control over our environment—the virtue of good design in our living quarters when it creates a sense of harmony and well-being is unmistakable.

Mary and Joan, for instance, are hopeful examples of a growing awareness of the importance of individual good taste. The realization that a tasteful environment is necessary to a full, pleasant life is relatively new, reflecting deep sociological, economic, and scientific changes of the last few decades. Mary, in her modest, free approach, and Joan, in her overpositive one, nevertheless make encouraging handwriting on the wall. We are learning that a concern with good taste is not affected or effeminate, but a vital basic need in our lives—now that we have the time to "soak it in." When we are no more self-conscious looking for it in a chair than in an automobile or a new dress, we will be close to being civilized. Then we will find that we spend more and more time at home, not because we have to, despite the many other places we might go, but because we find it the most enjoyable place.

Man's contemporary needs and economic limitations, plus a craving for a creditable background, have evolved today's house.

The section of the country we live in should indicate our setting. The kind of living possible in most of California nearly all year, for example, is restricted to a few months in other parts of the United States. A typical colonial house—two-storied, its roof pitched for snow, its windows limited, furnished in the style of its period—makes little sense where the climate and casual way of living call for the antithesis. The same house in Connecticut might be excellent.

Floor coverings, upholstery materials, curtains, and furniture should be controlled by where you live and what is practical in that setting. The indoor-outdoor life looks attractive in the magazines with all those bronzed, handsome people frolicking in the patio, and maybe it is good if the weather is mild and the air is not full of kamikaze mosquitoes.

A house should reflect the habits of the inhabitants, whether they are claustrophobiacs or claustromaniacs. How many people plan their living room for living? How many others materialize it out of the ectoplasmic life they picture themselves

. . . a house should reflect the habits of the inhabitants . . .

living? Should entertaining be forced feeding for the ego or fun for our friends? Should "looks" be sacrificed to comfort, or the reverse? Are we living in a way that's a struggle to maintain our financial equilibrium, or constantly postponing enjoyment of life till we get "just a little more saved up"? Are we living our own lives or those someone has designed for us?

Let's look at the Joneses—members of the "prominent set" in town. Once in a while they give a "formal dinner." It is now 1 A.M. and the hired maid has just closed the door on the last guest. We find madame aching with fatigue from the preparations, the party, and the new foundation that made it possible to get into that small-sized evening dress purchased for the occasion. The look of the good host fades from Jones's face, they both let out a constrained breath and gasp simultaneously, "Thank goodness. That's over!" She kicks off her shoes and Jones stumbles upstairs tearing off his coat and hard-boiled shirt as he goes.

In six hours, more or less, all evidences of punctilious housekeeping have been reduced to a mess. Did the flame of friendship ever burn in these dead ashes? Did the spirit of hospitality ever inhabit this shattered room? The flowers have bowed their wilted heads, there are liquor rings on what were highly polished tables, some of the coasters have been used for ash trays and are ruined. A glass of crème de menthe was spilled on the rose damask sofa when old Harry was cutting up; it will never be the same again. Harry's a scream, and if the party hadn't been formal he would have performed in the rumpus room and no harm done—except perhaps to Harry. His fall in the living room was cushioned by a thick carpet. On the tile floor downstairs he might have broken his neck. When Jones begins to tote up the damage he may wish Harry had.

After hearing the price of the wife's new dress, Jones had balked at replacing his ten-year-old tux, though he'd put on a couple of inches around the waist lately and it was damned uncomfortable. Every time he has to throw one of these wing-dings it costs him plenty. There are all sorts of unthought-of expenses that pop up at the last minute. The dishes, for instance —as far as Jones can see, the kitchen cupboards are loaded with "crockery," but when you give one of these formal dinners everything's got to be just right. So they added to their best china set. When she was downtown doing that, the wife saw a pair of porcelain birds that would really dress up the table. They weren't cheap. New cocktail glasses and sheer little napkins, costly for anything so small, were bought. And since "everything should match," sherry and cordial glasses were added. On top of those extras, figure the food, liquor, cut flowers, and orchids for the wife, with other expenses that he's forgotten at the moment. It's easy to see that Jones is in the hole for about half a grand.

Was it worth it? Jones always sleeps badly after mixing cocktails, wine, and rich food, and will be in a fine frenzy tomorrow. His office force will need all their tact to placate him. Mrs. Jones is cross and tired and it will take her several days to return to her easygoing normal self. An evening like this always promises to be fun when Mrs. Jones first issues the invitations and begins dreaming up the menu. Little pictures run through her mind of gracious, candlelit rooms, witty conversation, exquisite food, handsome men and beautifully dressed women, and she, the expert hostess, gently in command of this enchanting evening. But alas, as this theatrical dream of glory waxes, the realities wane. She sees things wrong with the setting where the play must take place. In an effort to set things right, last-minute props are introduced, and for the leading lady, a new costume. At last, and too soon, the fateful hour arrives. No one can say she hasn't done her best, but it just isn't good enough. It doesn't go off as she had pictured it. It never has, and when she allows herself to give way she thinks perhaps it never will. But that mood passes too, and next time Mrs. Jones will be just as optimistic, frantic, and disappointed. What made her party the dull, amateurish comedy of errors instead of the sophisticated, sparkling *divertissement* she had planned?

Mrs. Jones's parties lack éclat principally because of their effort at formality. She is coddling the foolish notion that formality is a Siamese twin to gracious living. This quaint myth is bruited about a good deal—in advertisements by manufacturers shaking sticks of imitation period furniture in the public's face, in editorial sections of magazines picturing elaborate mansions of prominent persons, in the society section of the local rag.

Few houses are properly equipped physically or staffed adequately for formal entertaining, and an attempt to pull off an elegantly correct gathering under too many handicaps is an excruciating effort that trusses up the evening into a turkey. Even those who have the means and a knack for formality are not always well advised to insist on this type of entertaining.

. . . those who have the means are not well-advised to insist on this . . .

The old-world aristocrats of the seventeenth and eighteenth centuries and the tycoons of the twentieth have nothing in common save, occasionally, the outward appearance of their domiciles. The gentleman of three centuries ago was a leisured creature to whom culture was a virtual profession. He was at home with the arts and social graces as Jones is at home in his fishing shack or automobile agency. The European aristocrat's most rugged pursuit was hunting. The silks, satins, and powdered wig he habitually wore were removed by a pack of lackeys, and, in leathern jacket, great boots, and befitting doodads, he was mounted on a handsomely caparisoned beast and enjoyed a few hours' murder of four-footed friends. On his return he was divested of the sturdy clothes, bathed, perfumed, and, resuming his fancy raiment, wandered down the grand staircase to the great hall where his elegant guests, after similar recreation, awaited him. They were disposed about the great apartment on chairs that nicely matched their showy but inhuman garb. They were busy improving the fine art of conversation. Time was the bauble of the leisured classes, and the cultivated graces throve in this orchid-house atmosphere. It was a life full of pretty affectations, and it was meet that these pampered few should live a life of pomp and ceremony in this background.

Today the master of the local château, whose income is a good deal more than Jones's, is seldom a connoisseur of the arts. He is often a generous subscriber to any community cause, be it the symphony or policemen's beanos. He has been too busy getting on in the world to have spent much time acquiring a cultural background. His education outside his own sphere is sketchy. Any hobby he rides is usually a favorite sport. He works a full day at least five days a week and keeps an early to bed, early to rise schedule—he keeps the hours of a lackey of the seventeenth or eighteenth century. Is this chap, in the twentieth-century rendition of a French château staffed by a motley crew of ever-changing faces, living his own life in these lofty rooms full of the most formal, splendid period furniture? The life of a European aristocrat of three hundred years ago? Or the life of Riley?

All the time the Joneses are grimly running the gamut of formality, exhausting their financial and physical resources, the folks in their "set," who are all hitting the same blue-blooded notes on their scale of living, are chasing in the same circle trying to keep up with the Joneses. This curious defect in our social fabric seems to be a carry-over from our economic mode. It is wise and good that we compete in business and the professions, for that keeps our economy free and on its toes. But competition has a very doubtful utility in our social or private lives. It may be the "life of trade," but it can turn our houses into chaotic comedies of bad taste. Why should anybody try to keep up with the Joneses? They are not going anywhere. They have been in a rut since the Ice Age!

Some of the home-furnishing magazines which stress snob appeal are largely responsible for inciting competition in our private lives. Snob appeal is sometimes laid on so heavily as to turn a strong stomach and at other times appears only as a mild suggestion. It is aimed at the Joneses and their disciples. It ballyhoos the surroundings and doings of those who appear in the *Social Register, Burke's Peerage,* and the Stork Club. We're all naturally curious to know how the more blue-blooded and red-blooded live. But do the magazines picture the homes of the famous to point out good taste? Look at some of the frightening piles belonging to the prominent. Is it "Gracious

Living," as the magazines say, or would it give you a touch of the screaming meemies? The magazines' editors would laugh at showing them if they belonged to "nobodies." Some of the homes of the highly placed are imaginative and beautiful, but their "important" names usually appeal to the editors even more than their fortunate good taste.

Pictorial display of the mansions of the rich or famous, surrounded by acres of magnificent gardens, is a social and esthetic scoop for a magazine but often discouraging to the average home and garden planner. Those estates, sometimes lovely indeed, are interesting, but living in this grandest sense is almost a lost art. An occasional picture of this kind of life can make us sigh for other days or congratulate ourselves on the ease and simplicity of our own way, but its overemphasis in the magazines is surely a lost cause.

Of course there are a few people who have the means and talent for living essentially in the grand manner, and if ease and familiarity are natural to their habit of living, they may well accomplish it pleasantly and gracefully. But these do not require our scrutiny.

Some, like the Joneses, are formal only occasionally, and others have learned that they can be themselves gracefully on all occasions. The home-furnishing magazines also devote much space to appropriate ways of living and entertaining informally. They picture tempting new ideas for interiors, outdoor living, and preparing and serving food. Many are excellent and deserve consideration. They point out that if your way of life is uncomfortable you aren't even living. If you have to batten yourselves down for the social storm, your guests will be uncomfortable too.

Is the living room by-passed for den, sun porch, or rumpus

room? If it is "dressy," "formal," it doesn't invite the use of the master returning from the marts of trade, the offspring in levis, or the mistress back from some experiments in the potting shed. If the living room is as uncomfortable as most so-called formal rooms, it doesn't welcome guests on the rare occasions when it is used. Nothing will incubate an egg as fast as an evening in an atmosphere full of uneasy chairs.

On a recent job a decorator ran into an unlivable-living-room problem. The client said the upstairs library was always used *en famille* and the living room only for entertaining; she thought it should be redone in the same style. He could more or less do as he liked about it; she was most interested in what the decorator suggested for the rest of the house, which everyone used and enjoyed. The decorator, however, was most concerned with the wasted, neglected living room. He kept it in its original style but modified it by adding comfortable seating arrangements, a warm color scheme which gave it a feeling of ease and attractiveness. Now the library is no longer crowded with the family and its intimates. The living room is the most popular place in the house, and for the purpose of entertaining it is far more pleasant than before.

The way things are done is more eloquent than what they're done with. The basic needs for entertaining are simple. A good time, like good taste, needn't cost much. Friends can have as much fun in a one-room apartment at a simple buffet supper as in a grand house at a six-course dinner. Putting on the dog and having a *dog*goned good time are the twain that seldom meet.

The trimmings or "glamour" side of housekeeping and entertaining can be booby traps for the uninitiated. Most houses have limited storage space, and anything that is used only occasionally is a nuisance. Why invest in an expensive set of china that's "saved" for "best" once or twice a year? It makes much better sense to have several kinds of china, earthenware, and pottery—not complete sets—which can be used for different courses or occasions, but used often. The same is true of solid-silver flatware and hollowware—if it is kept jacketed in felt, what good is it? Unless several wines are served with dinner, a large assortment of glassware is an extravagance. One type of glass can serve for three or four, and the money saved will buy a better quality plus a few good decanters and pitchers. Costly linens can be more of a liability than an asset. For less than the price of an expensive, hand-embroidered cloth that must be laundered each time it's used, there are many hand-woven table mats that will be as effective and twice as serviceable. If you are caught short by that "formal" occasion when you think you must have a gold-banded set of china, silver coffee urn, six different kinds of glasses, call in a good caterer! He can supply all you need, handle everything correctly, and then mosey along, taking all that stuff with him.

To some, a bar in the house is a prime necessity. This doesn't necessarily mean that they're candidates for Alcoholics Anonymous. It may be an efficient way of handling their entertaining or, used as an ice-cream bar, of maintaining a high standing with the teen-age set. But before setting up an altar to Bacchus, it's a good idea to consider that very likely the master of the ménage is going to find himself behind it, officiating in a semiprofessional capacity. Some men enjoy this sort of thing and in the case of a big blowout will cheerfully hire someone with a union card to handle those jokers who ask for complex libations. If this isn't your idea of fun, your guests can get just as well

95

. . . officiating in a
semi-professional capacity . . .

oiled making their own drinks from a tray of fixings set up on some convenient table.

The "reform" school of thought popular at present decrees that most dining rooms are a vestigial remain and must go because the days of endless hearty repasts are no more. However, a dining room is probably a necessity for large families and desirable for small ones who dislike buffet suppers and enjoy giving frequent dinner parties. But living-room dining is suitable and pleasant in many houses and can be done with "style" as well as informality. And no one need apologize for kitchen dining if the setting is attractive. It is a matter as individual as the question of the necessary number and type of bedrooms.

Some couples, whose sleeping habits are diverse, should certainly have separate bedrooms if they are to maintain the same address. For a small increase in building cost, two small bedrooms can be managed in place of one that is spacious. Bed-sitting rooms are a reasonable answer to some problems. Two of them plus a bath and good-sized kitchen are an interesting idea for small-family living.

What is the general living pattern? The family's main interest? For what are the various rooms in the house most often used? What are the points of contention and how can they be avoided? Is there a bridge game nearly every evening and no one to play the piano? Have a good-looking permanent card table and chairs set up in the living room and hock the baby grand. Do the young people tear up the room for dancing every time they get together? Do away with the heavy, precise furniture and carpet in favor of small, light tables and chairs which can be easily pushed away and rugs that can be tossed aside. The children will be housekeeping on their own in a few years, and the "old folks" can have everything their way then. Does the living room bulge with dreary, overstuffed furniture? Comfort is certainly important, but an equal amount of ease can be accomplished with smaller pieces that look well and can be re-arranged for conversations and flirtations. Comfort need not be sacrificed to "looks"—they can be complementary and ideally occur together.

When the house is "redone" the old man may put up a violent squawk against getting rid of "his chair," a gaucherie in the new scheme, but it "suits his back." Work out a compromise with him; get a suitable new cover for his chair. Or, if he'll be even more reasonable, find a good-looking easy chair that will suit him and the house too. Don't become so effete that his pipe rack begins to look "incorrect." He lives here too! Unless you're willing to make some concessions to your mate's comfort and well-being, he may begin spending all his time in the den, workshop, office, or club, and no jury would convict him!

. . . get a chair that will suit him . . .

The customer on the prowl for one piece of furniture or a houseful will encounter some "help" from salesmen and home furnishers. Until, perhaps bewildered by it all, he puts his head between the lion's choppers and talks to a "home consultant" or hires a decorator.

Many of these characters feel that they know what's best for you much better than you do yourself; they got this way because they have been told that they have "such a flair," "such good taste." This flattery is further bolstered by the unhappy circumstance that the average customer's taste is often very bad indeed. Most of these so-called decorators and "consult-

TISK - TISK

. . . if we could only throw everything out . . .

ants" are little more than floor salesmen, and whether on salary or in a tiny nook of their own, they trot their customers through store or wholesale house recommending the "best things." On their first visit to your modest villa, which you've always thought had a certain charm, they will wander through it shaking their heads. Finally they may sigh, "If we could only throw everything out." We seldom can, even if willing to take this desperate expedient, so they reconcile themselves to "doing the best they can with it."

Fortunately there are salesmen, furnishers, and decorators whose horizons are wider, who try to help the client find the best way to live his own life. Decorators, more aptly called interior designers, often have an impressive background with an art training based on practicality as well as esthetics. Many of them are professional draftsmen, at home with period and contemporary styles, and often have a working knowledge of several handicrafts. They are equipped to start at the drawing board and create the whole scheme for any type of room or house or do an original interpretation. Many of the jobs these designers handle are tailor-made for their individual customers' needs and ideas. Usually with the competence necessary for this kind of decorating goes a tolerant understanding of pleasing the client on a long-range basis. They have their troubles with the public. It is difficult for most non-professionals to visualize from a drawing what a chair, table, or room will eventually look and feel like in reality. Interior designers are used to having their clients in a fine frenzy of indecision when the work has reached the final scheme stage, when drawings in

98

color are finished and the job is ready to be built. A client may feel that her specially designed room looks oddly unfamiliar, although it represents her demands and real desires. Perhaps now a number of minor changes that soon become major take place. The client begins to get rattled, and she wakes up in the night asking herself why she insisted on that love seat. Meanwhile the designer, an old hand at this hot-and-cold game, is asking himself what lunatic twist of fate got him into this business anyhow. In this phase the designer is inclined to be irritable with the stock clerk whose dream it is to enter this wrath race. But if the customer isn't more difficult than most, and the designer is good, the result is usually a happy one for both. The client will get a comfortable, workable, attractive house and the designer a new friend who will recommend him to others.

It is no compliment to say that a room looks as if it has been "decorated." Most often this means that it lacks personality and individuality, is brand new and a trite bore. There are few personal touches to distinguish it from an arrangement in a shopwindow. No designer can supply these. He can, however, create a setting to suit the client and his family that will be different from any other.

A few years ago a house was being readied for an important customer. The decorator finished his work as her ship was docking a few miles away. It was an attractive, out-of-ordinary scheme; everything was as he had planned it to the final details, to plants and flowers in the right places. He took a last look and felt that it lacked something. After the client moved in it was exactly right; she had added a few intimate, personal touches— treasured ornaments, favorite pictures and photographs, books and magazines. It had become a charming, comfortable house belonging to an individual. It did not look as if it had been "done," or, as many houses do, "done in" by a decorator.

The butterfly, railroad print, or china dog collection so near your heart needn't be hidden from the decorator and brought into the open after he has departed. He can help you fit it into the plan. Unless the client's ideas are too cockeyed or the decorator has an overblown conception of his "artistic integrity," he will try to be co-operative.

A recent customer, an enthusiastic big-game fisherman, insisted that his most prized trophy, a giant marlin, be mounted over the fireplace in his bedroom. The decorator was co-operative, and the result is surprisingly excellent. The huge fish is a startling but interesting decoration, and doubtless the captor of the piscatorial wonder recalls the great day, full of sunshine, excitement, and triumph, every time he looks at it. A suitable background attractively arranged is the goal, and if it can be merged with the things that delight, is there a better way of living?

Consider the reaction of another brass hat of big business. He needed a picture for his sitting room. It seemed fitting to suggest that, since he was an avid golfer and some of his happiest hours were spent at the club, a handsome water color could be chosen from an excellent show of landscapes that included several of golf courses. Unexpectedly, the customer thought the suggestion silly. He bought instead an English sporting print full of foxhounds and pink-coated gentlemen splendidly mounted, all "foreigners."

Occasionally, in the houses of friends, we are embarrassed by the feeling that they are out of character with their owners. Often, grim evidences of fond memories of things past are allowed to remain, fouling up the current scene because their owners have got used to them or lack the courage to evict them. There are country houses that have the formality of town houses, beach houses so furnished as to repel the intent for which they were built. There are people living in Southern mansions in the Middle West, Cape Cod houses in California, Spanish Colonial *casas* in the East, not to mention the mongrels all over the country called English, French, Italian, and Spanish styles—furnished and decorated with dingbats many and various.

It takes a bit of believing, but the information comes from an unpixyish source that there is a rushing business at present in the sale of fake television antennas! A good many people evidently want to appear to be on the beam. Nor are these citizens necessarily characters. Beside the curious pretenses by which many civilized people live their lives, the voodoos and hoodoos of those we call savages seem reasonable and intelligent.

There are a good many socio-economic factors that are helping to form the patterns of our lives. As wages go up in the building trades, as costs rise in the manufacture of household furnishings and decoration and in the market of domestic help, our houses must become smaller, simpler, our household effects fewer, many of them made of new and more useful materials. They must be well arranged and easy to care for; everything we live with must count for much in economy, utility, and good looks.

We may not be able in our time to know if the reasons for the changes are all good. But, used well, the changes can be very good indeed. In a complicated world more Americans can live more simply, easily, with greater privacy and freedom, in more attractive surroundings, than they ever did before.

101

Tricks of the Trade

Pick up any of the home-furnishing magazines—the source of the average person's ideas of taste and style. It's a sandwich consisting of plenty of crust surrounding a layer of food for thought. Since the magazine contains vastly more advertising material than editorial advice, it misleads even the wariest customer. From full-page layouts in color to small black-and-white cuts, thousands of promotions clamor for your attention in a glib sort of gibberish: "Classic Victorian," "Gracious Provincial," "Beautiful Traditional," "Designer Styled," "Flexi-Hexi," "Heirloom Elegance," "Southern Romance." In this same jargon manufacturers hawk their wares in trade journals for the edification of the home-furnishing stores. Millions are spent yearly to reiterate this mumbo-jumbo. Many of the products advertised are as bogus as the copy. Look at some of them.

. . . pick up any home-furnishing magazine . . .

Most of the period called "Victorian" was conspicuous for erratic design. Absurd even in its own day, do copies of it vulgarly emblazoned with machine carving make sense? Yet several manufacturers are busy reviving its horrors.

. . . an excellent country piece from France . . .

In La Belle France there are many regional or provincial styles. Some of these antique country pieces are excellent, some preposterous. Any hillbilly could recognize the unique style of each province. As a change from the familiar and meaningless "Provincial" on the market, a competent designer, using as inspiration line, scale, and decoration suggested by a few of the finer genuine examples, could enrich the market with some sincere interpretations. But Provincial misunderstood by the average American manufacturer and his customers is hardly reminiscent of the genuine design types from rural France.

There is a conglomerate mass of Grand Rapids stuff that is built on a let-George-do-it idea—George I, II, III, and IV, that is. This product haphazardly borrows line and embellishment from the genuine article. Most of it, selling in the medium-priced brackets in deep red mahogany suites, is aggrandized by mass-produced inlay. The more expensive lines in this style show good craftsmanship but give the same effect of monotonous repetition and crushing boredom whether in simple cottage or pretentious manse. There are thousands of acres of it stretching from coast to coast.

Some of the "Modern" furniture that can be bought in different units for assembly in a variety of ways uses the "flexi-hexi" type of "personalized construction" as a selling gimmick. Most customers are satisfied to use it in its more reasonable standard arrangements, though the possibilities of its combinations are probably its basic appeal. The names given many spooks masquerading as modern-styled furniture as well as the excellently designed contemporary groups are so weird that it is risky to fabricate an unlikely name for the purpose of referring to them, for fear someone has already dreamed it up to publicize a new line.

At the other end of the manufacture of modern designs is the "borax" product. "Borax," a term well understood in the trade, applies to any furniture that is made to look larger than life and to seem what it isn't. The usable space, most expensive to construct in chest or divan, is cut down under minimum requirements. The surfaces of the arms, legs, backs, and sides of the pieces are expanded with inexpensive hollow-wall construction. The trimmings, upholstery, and hardware are flashier, fancier, bigger. Most "borax" is low priced, though there are a few exceptions up in the money. But the attraction is the same. To the average customer a "borax" piece will have what the manufacturer calls "eye appeal"; it looks like "a lot for the money." He trades on a typical American thinking habit, that biggest and best are synonymous—biggest building, biggest car, biggest fortune, biggest all-star cast. . . .

a lot for the money . . .

. . borax . . .

105

Provincial, Traditional, Early American, and Modern are long-established trade names for a catholic variety of furniture types on the American market. "Chinese Modern," an outgrowth of early chop-suey, has become another trade name used to identify a heterogeneous collection owing little inspiration to the artisans of Cathay. Some years ago one factory started making a line that was generally well-conceived and reminiscent of certain Chinese designs. It was successful, and soon other manufacturers brought out their "interpretations." The mishmash results acquired "face" by being called "Chinese Modern." When fabrics mills, ceramics factories, lamp manufacturers, and radio-cabinet makers began to cash in on the trend, "Chinese Modern" had as little resemblance to the meaning of its name as a laughing hyena has to a chow.

. . . early chop-suey . . .

The semantics of the home-furnishings trade are amusingly ephemeral. Names that seem to hint at basic meanings often are the result of a hasty christening to legitimize an illicit design. In time they are accepted as significant definitions for all sorts of orphans. Customers, as innocent of knowledge as most of the salesmen who wait on them, soon learn that furni-

ture called "Traditional" means mahogany; that "Provincial," made of light wood and dark wood, is "French"; that "Early American" is maple or cherry; and "Modern"—well, everybody knows "Modern" when they see it. Even these inept classifications may soon disappear. Some furniture salesmen are approaching the customers with a blunt, "Do you want to see 'Modern' or mahogany?"

A casual inspection of the bunko pitches used to sell fabrics, carpets, silver, glass, china, linens, decorative objects, and gift-wares reveals that they are as empty of meaning as are many of the things they sell. What are they supposed to mean? "Classic"—eons of bastardization of original designs? "Heirloom" —falsifications of the past? "Designer-styled," "High fashion colors"—antidotes for confused customers or adrenalin for the market? "Traditional"—the tradition of buying what the manu-facturers call traditional? "Southern Romance"—a marriage of convenience with the ante-bellum days? What's the gag? Why all this foxy double talk? What does it accomplish? Well, it sells the goods!

Let us take a few looks at the squirrel run of the United States market by getting to know Horace. Though typical, he is not intended to serve as an example of all American furniture manufacturers, for many are people of taste and acumen, as attested by their products. But as for Horace and his ilk . . .

107

To his family, friends, and the people he does business with, Horace is a swell egg. To his critics—you and me—he's a champion layer of same. He turns out a volume line of medium-priced "period" furniture called the Lady Baltimore Gracious Living Group. He's been doing this for years with great success. Horace doesn't know beans when the bag's open about the period characterized by George I to VI or the original designs indigenous to rural France. Why should he? If he decides to add a new piece to his line, he will leaf through some sketches, or glance at one or two books on period furniture, or study the catalogues of his competitors, or even go so far as to look at an authentic piece. But despite the "inspiration" used, changes will be made—to give it a "different" look, to avoid a charge of copycat, and above all to bring down production costs. So, regardless of the design source, the piece produced by Horace, with its lines and proportions altered, will be thrown a little out of joint. The changes deemed necessary nearly always destroy the combination that gave the original its characteristic style. Horace will thus achieve a hit or mystery that may be incorporated in a bedroom suite advertised as "Gorgeous Georgian." If you ask Horace what that means he'll think you're pretty thick. If you ask him if he thinks it is good-looking he'll think you're crazy. Popping such a question to himself has never occurred to him. He's in the furniture business, isn't he? And he hasn't got time for any of "that arty monkey business."

Perhaps this year Horace decides to give his business a shot in the arm. He hires a big-name designer, the elegant Wedge-leigh Trimm, to do a "prestige" line for him. The knowing Trimm belongs to that small coterie so often pictured in the "class" decorating magazines, impeccably groomed, languidly at ease in a smart interior of his own contriving. His services are first-class and costly, but Horace is no fool and knows the investment is solid gold. One day Trimm delivers the finished drawings, collects his fee, and with visions of future royalties fades. Horace will not tamper with these designs. He tools up a small corner of his factory and summons his advertising man, Blitzen, of Blitzen, Don-

. . . Horace decides to give his business a shot in the arm . . .

ner & Blitzen. This clever chap will go to almost any lengths to please Horace, his most valued account. Blitzen knows much less of the furniture business than does Horace, who at least understands production. It is Blitzen who fits all the hifalutin' customer-catching phrases together.

Horace and Blitzen concentrate their heavy artillery on the name and fame of Trimm, the designer. When the advertising campaign is complete, Horace himself takes it to the magazines chosen to feature it. The advertising department will be in a steam of appreciation, Horace will expand in the deference accorded him. When the editor is called in to see the campaign there will be more felicitations. Ordinarily the editor does not look forward to Horace's occasional appearances, but now that Horace has the Wedgeleigh Trimm line in tow the editor will gladly get behind it with a big story and illustrations. He can repeat his well-worn protest with authority this time: "The magazine does not promote advertisers unless their products have unusual merit and their presentation is a service to our readers, in line with our policy." This is: the Trimm line is good-looking, fresh, and the prestige of the designer's name will give it snob appeal.

With the campaign ready, and the models coming off the production line, Horace alerts the store buyers. He sends out an impressive announcement of a "consultation" to his most important accounts. Actually the "consultation" will be nothing more than a preview but will butter up the buyers from the retail stores by inferring that the line awaits their valued approval before it is put on the market. The merchandise managers of the stores chosen for this compliment will O.K. the buyers' special trips because their stores can afford it; Wedgeleigh Trimm is a well-known designer; Horace is "important in the trade"—they've all been selling his Lady Baltimore line successfully for years; because as leading stores they must scoop their competitors; and, finally, because they will share prestige advertising, partially paid for by Horace.

The majority of the buyers who attend the "consultation" couldn't tell a good design from a bad one. They are all under constant pressure from their merchandise managers to do a "volume business," so whatever turns over the fastest is naturally the best from their point of view.

When Horace has his carefully culled guests and his regional representatives corralled in the show ring, he brings out the mavericks. At first the buyers are a little cagey. It is customary procedure to play hard to get. Anyhow, they're here to be consulted, aren't they? All right, then, let's consult. Horace and his salesmen don't make heavy weather of this temporary cold front. They know the fluctuations in temperature of these votaries of volume sales. Horace's accomplices are enthusiastic fellows and must retain a lighthearted ebullience, for it is to their interest and natural to their kind to believe what the manufacturer says.

After a pause for lunch peppered with double martinis and *double-entendres*—back to the showroom. The atmosphere is warmer. In the air of geniality the buyers begin to appreciate the Trimm line. They are, of course, anxious to sew it up for their territory, and no one is more aware of this than Horace. Some one or two more erudite in the group may appreciate the excellence of the designs, and say so. But if there are any doubters—because the Trimm line looks unfamiliar and therefore seems a bit risky—it is not likely they will mention it. They know the furniture will have plenty of promotion—almost a guarantee of success with the public; a good many of the things they've been doubtful about in the past they've bought anyhow for the same reason. And the threat is always implied, "So-and-so wants it in your territory. We're offering it to you first because you've always been one of our favorite accounts." The fellow on this spot casts himself into the future for a moment; imagines it a wild success in his competitor's store and his merchandise manager's understandable wrath. These uneasy characters spending their stores' money with studied uncertainty also attach a good deal of importance to being "well liked in the trade." This springs from a natural urge to be popular and the knowledge that when things are tight in times of short supply a buyer with a long history of playing ball gets first consideration.

. . . his merchandise manager's wrath . . .

Now, Horace does not sell them; he tells them. He tells them that this is a package deal—they can have the line for a minimum purchase of five thousand dollars' worth; also they must devote a thousand square feet of store space to featuring it and follow the promotion campaign that has been planned. It's a deal.

The next move takes place during market week, when manufacturers display their wares for the trade. Most furniture buyers attend this market, and many are attracted to Horace's

111

display because the news of the Trimm line has spread through the trade. Some of them can do no more than look at it, for Horace has already given it to their competitors, or it may be too "high-styled" for their stores. Horace will guide these lesser lights to Lady Baltimore, a known quantity at half the price. The Trimm line will be the honeypot that attracts scores of drones from stores all over the country, but the "period" furniture will land their orders. More of these models will be sold than ever before with the Trimm lure.

It was not a part of the master plan, but Horace has done the public a service in promoting the well-designed, well-made furniture created by Trimm. It is worth the price to those who buy it; it serves as a good example of contemporary style to those who do not; it encourages the same sort of production by other manufacturers and the chance that the market will eventually be able to offer fine modern furniture in a modest price bracket.

Horace is no zany. After the successful test of the Trimm line, which boosted his business and for a "class" product didn't sell too badly, Horace will prepare to throw a curve which, with the suave parabola of a boomerang, will return the cost of promotion a thousandfold. Horace will get together a line of modern furniture by doing a little "research" on the competitive market, by incorporating a few ideas from the Trimm line—still kept in small production—and perhaps even by flipping through the pages of a book on "modern." As in the "period" line, inexpensive construction will dictate design.

Blitzen will dream up a name for the new product. The Superban line it will be called. An excellent name for higgledy-piggledy, inexpensive modern furniture. It suggests top quality, informal country living, and modernity. Horace will allocate a big section of his factory to handle this production. He will gamble that it will be a volume seller. He will promote all three lines at once, Lady Baltimore, Trimm, and Superban. Trimm's name will again be heavily stressed, and the motto "Horace-Crafted" will be prominent in the national advertising campaign.

The editors of the home-furnishing magazines will try to steer clear of Horace when he drops around to get some free space for the Superban line. It won't be up to their standard. But as a compromise they will offer to illustrate the Trimm line again. This will be okay with Horace. He'll have three balls in the air which he can juggle indefinitely. Roughly, this is the windup: the Superban and Trimm lines—because both are "Modern," both are made by the same factory and are pictured side by side in promotions—become confused in the minds of the trade and the public. The Superban line has taken on some of the prestige of the Trimm line and it is much, much cheaper.

Horace has perpetrated no fraud. When a store buyer enters his showroom the salesman may say, "That table was designed by Trimm," or, pointing to a Superban piece near by, "Another 'Horace-Crafted' design," and will go on to quote the reasonable price. There's an association that identifies the Horace product of modern furniture as one of the best on the market, as the Trimm line is. Unless the buyer is an exception, he will infer that the Superban line is a much better value than the Trimm line; it will turn over four times faster! The store sales force will react as the buyer did; they will be aided and abetted by the public who, through the great publicity campaign put on by Horace, will associate the poor furniture with the good furniture and will clamor for it. Horace will be deluged by orders.

Horace, his confederates and peers are practical people and recognize that their fellow Americans are too. If he and his alter egos in the trade could open their eyes to the necessity for an equal amount of know-how in the drafting room, the problem of achieving good taste might be solved. In other fields of manufacture this expedient reaps a handsome harvest. Good looks generally distinguish our automobiles, refrigerators, stoves, and other appliances. The manufacturers of these have learned to trust the designs of their products to specialists just as they make engineers responsible for their functions. Every product of all-around excellence has two things in common: a crackerjack designer and a boss who trusts his designer's ability. The factories that produce inferior furniture, rugs, fabrics, tableware, gifts, and what not have two things in common: a frustrated designer and an egocentric boss who insists on the last word in the drafting room. Although by hiring a designer he has admitted that he himself is not qualified, he can't resist adding a few touches of his own. Esthetically, the kiss of death; unfortunately, not often moribund from the standpoint of sales.

Sometimes the appearance of a superior product in a mediocre lot may be due to chance. Several years ago a Scandinavian silversmith introduced a flatware pattern. Later an American factory brought out a design that closely resembled the original. It became a sensational success. The public got a fine design in silver by accident. It was not lifted because the manufacturer had analyzed its excellence. It was merely a heist in the dark.

Horace's counterparts are found in every country functioning on the law of supply and demand. There are many foreign factories even now busily concocting designs that in the 1890s

. . . useful . . .

were *à la mode*. They are still doing pretty well, to our shame, but they are unable to understand why our demand for their burlesques has declined, that tastes have changed, and that the cutting off of the foreign market for years at a time causes many things to be forgotten and, when seen again by a new generation of nest builders, to be found wanting. One European manufacturer made it his business to learn what the discriminating American public wants, then hired one of his country's great designers to create a line of pure white porcelain dinnerware. The shapes are useful and beautiful, the price is reasonable, the volume and turnover immense.

. . . beautiful . . .

. . . reasonable . . .

. . . steered onto the
rocks by captains of industry . .

Many businesses have been steered onto the rocks by captains of industry who thought that merchandising one kind of thing was much like another. A well-known example concerns a small factory managed by a designer that produced a limited quantity of excellent furniture. It got a great amount of free publicity in the editorial sections of the home-furnishing magazines. The editors were pleased to single it out because it was excellent and had few competitors. As a result, the demand outgrew the capacity of the factory, and a large manufacturer who used the same materials in the fabrication of a low-priced volume line bought the designer-owner out. Unfortunately for all concerned, including the public, the excellent furniture was so mishandled that sales began to diminish and it was finally taken off the market. The big manufacturer was used to promoting a strictly commercial product. He had no understanding of the superior furniture, the reasons for its superiority, or how it must be represented to the buying public.

Manufacturers in all branches of the home-furnishings trade, backed by their million-dollar promotions, are far more potent influences on our physical and mental habits, our emotions and tastes than all we may learn through schools, libraries, galleries, or museums. For they provide us with that first fount of impressions, the home environment. They are the basic caterers of our culture, and whether we are to be cretins or creatures of refinement depends on our choice of their wares.

It is a fact that there is enough merchandise in all price brackets, of all types of household furnishings on the market, that is excellent. There are a few departments in stores throughout the country that reflect this good taste. Their buyers shop in the same markets as their competitors, but the contrast between a department of well-selected merchandise and those without taste or thought is so shocking one would believe that the sources were completely different. It is not surprising that most of us dread the advent of the Christmas season and the attendant struggle to find a few gifts possible to present with a feeling of good will toward men. At no time is it more obvious that most of the unhappy objects masquerading as decorative articles and giftwares have been palmed off on incompetent store buyers somnambulating through merchandise marts. The suffering clerks at the return desk would not be on the verge of nervous breakdowns if the buyers were able to apply some sensible thought to the ultimate use and artistic worth of their purchases.

Why are there so many booby traps offered for sale? Because the average selection is based on what the factory salesman says. This dodge came into being when the last peddler folded his pack and faded away. Let us open *Harper's Magazine* of September 1868: "During the last thirty years the industry of the country has been emerging from the condition represented by the word *shop* to the height and amplitude indicated by the word *manufactory.*

. . . buyers somnambulating through merchandise marts . . .

Every thing is getting to be done on the grand scale. The solitary peddler, trudging along over the hills with his pack, has given place to the alert, accomplished Agent, who represents a great Company, travels in the cars, lodges in splendid hotels, regales his customer with turtle and Champagne, and sells more goods in one transaction than the peddler did in a lifetime."

This is the way it is still done: "Look at these," today's agent boasts, riffling the pages of the order book under the buyer's nose. "Biggest seller I've had in years!" He points out objects in silver, or china, glassware, linen, or gifts that are as likely to be candidates for the funny papers as pleasant additions to the home. The public has not seen them but they are "the biggest sellers in years"—to the stores. Will the public ask for them? Indubitably: they are intensively promoted; factory salestalk will be repeated all the way down the line until it reaches the receptive ears of the customers. Thus everybody is finally cuckolded by the hucksters hired by the manufacturers. The drumbeats acquire a hypnotic credence by the time they have filtered through the trade. To the advertising agent, busy dreaming up these fancies, it's all in a day's work. He is saying the same things for lots of other products in as many different ways as his invention can supply.

Why is the average store buyer a stranger to good taste? Consider his background: he may have started as a clever salesman or might have been a law or medical student who lost interest, heart, or out, and then drifted into merchandising, where personality is so often mistaken for ability. Or, like many, perhaps he has risen to eminence through the more menial jobs in a store—packer, checker, stock boy, record keeper. Seniority, a factor in promotion, is often one with obsolescence, so when the lucky chap inherits the job of buyer his ways are set.

A major chore of every buyer is to see that his department's records are carefully kept. They make the difference between success and failure. A talented lad with the records seldom goes unsung or unrewarded. He is carefully nursed along, encouraged with an occasional raise until he becomes assistant buyer. As assistant, he must think and act as much like his boss as possible. He gets acquainted with the trade and the market in the way his mentor knows it and learns to have the same taste and judgment. After a decade or so he tumbles into the spot he's been prepared for and finds himself as much of a square in a round hole as his predecessor.

Most buyers will obviously choose an assistant who has an intelligence and education comparable, not superior, to their own; so when the time comes for the protégés to take over, the caliber of talent will not be improved. With the constant repetition of this system there is seldom a change for the better, but a duplication of the same sad lack of fitness for the job.

If an assistant becomes impatient he may get a chance to purchase goods at another store where they "need someone with his background"—the same trackless desert of ideas that exists in the mind of his former boss and probably in the marble head of the man he is replacing.

The buyer usually gets a share of profits, and so avoids taking chances with unfamiliar merchandise or improvements on familiar stock, but bets the store's money year after year on "sure things." Since his knowledge of esthetic value is limited, worth-while new merchandise is rarely given a break. Most of the new lines bought in small supply are selected on the basis of a familiar look or a factory representative's persuasive salesmanship. If a new line doesn't sell at once, the salespeople are pressured with, "It's funny you haven't been successful with this merchandise; it's selling like hot cakes everywhere else." The innocent customer is then told that it's taking the country by storm. If this doesn't turn the trick, little money has been laid out, and the merchandise can be used to sweeten the semi-annual sale when the buyer will retrieve his costs on the few bad bets he has made and also get some traffic in the department that will boom business in popular lines.

Store buyers have their favorite markets. Oddly enough, many in the West prefer to trek East in time to catch the Broadway shows, and their eastern confreres find an excuse to trip West in the season when golf courses are frozen at home, although both of them often have adequate sources for the things they need near by. A southern factory off the circuit but near Louisville got out of the red by giving the yearly preview during Derby Week.

One impressionable impresario of merchandise read in a popular illustrated weekly that the girls in Dallas packed more pulchritude than any others in the United States. A few months later his store featured a Rancho rumpus room that bore the Texas brand.

When American merchandisers shop in foreign markets their careless capers and lack of taste are as discouragingly obvious. In Italy a small group of buyers had already "made the market." The Italian factory salesmen were eager to show another American buyer what his countrymen had selected, thinking that he too would want the same things. Almost without exception this buyer found the choices to be the poorest examples, although there were plenty of fine designs available. If you asked a person of taste to pick out the worst from those displays, he would choose virtually the same objects that had been selected to thrust on the American public. As a result of the caliber of talent sent abroad, the customers at home are usually offered the dregs of foreign markets. A trip to the south of Italy will disclose that the charming, primitive designs characteristic of the region near Amalfi have been schmaltzed almost beyond recognition by the irresponsible demands of U.S. buyers. To find a cheaper source of manufacture, they brought samples of delicate, sophisticated French designs and had them copied. The Italian potters did not understand the unfamiliar patterns, unsuitable for their talents and materials. The results are cheap botches that will stand a high markup, and a fine native craft has been lost.

Any merchandiser, whether he has good taste or none, knows business success depends upon accurate record-keeping—to adjust the inventory to customer demands. But however well kept the records may be, or how often consulted, misinterpreting them is as hopeless as consulting the navel and can lead to business failure. A number of years ago costume pictures were tabu in Hollywood. "They're too expensive to produce," "The public doesn't want 'em," "They won't sell," the cinema czars said. One of the most powerful men in the industry braved this dictum and made a fortune at the box office. Immediately other studios followed suit. A few imitations were successes, most were flops. These arbiters of the public's taste in entertainment had misinterpreted its demands. The quality, not the type of product, attracted the public's spending power.

The "package deal" is a popular means of insuring volume sales. Designers and manufacturers combine their talents to create a group of furnishings that are to be shown together and presented to the customer in such a way as to make him feel that it must be all or nothing. A promising experiment was tried a few years ago. It comprised a furniture group, floor coverings, and a selection of draperies and upholstery fabrics in a generous color choice, plus lamps and decorative accessories. An integrated scheme of contemporary style that required only the purchase price to answer the furnishing problem. It was not a lasting success, as it had to be a little too high priced for the middle-bracket customer, its natural consumer. A package like this for the right price could be a valuable contribution.

There are more complex package deals in which high profits are assured. One or two completed houses in a new tract are decorated by a popular-priced furniture store, and the realty agent uses them to entice prospective customers. When he sells a house to a couple without household possessions, he notifies the store to send a salesman, who sells the furniture and ties up the package. The real-estate agent gets a cut from the store, the salesman a commission, and the customers have only to hang up their hats in the house and call it home. This deal is usually bought on a time-payment plan and seems a good value, and may be—if bought for cash. But a few fandangos with the interest rate can send it soaring. There are furniture stores that will sell only on time, to take advantage of hidden profits. These outfits are not licensed as pawnbrokers but as retail furniture stores!

The manufacturers of home furnishings believe they're operating at a profit because they have unlocked the secret of "what the public wants." How true is this? Do the public's demands mold the market or is a market demand created that molds the public?

Sometimes home-furnishing magazines are responsible for a trend. Several months before publication they notify wholesalers and retailers that an issue will feature a certain style —Regency, perhaps. Plans include articles showing several houses done in the period, owned by well-known people, and a number of authentic pieces and good copies. Regency is the news of the year. Manufacturers will use advertising space in the issue to promote their "period" lines, and many will hasten to bring things out in their peculiar interpretation of

Regency, which the stores will buy in advance of the issue to be ready for the trend which will hit the public like an avalanche. Salespeople will tell their customers that Regency is the "newest, smartest thing." And everyone who has hopped on the band wagon will congratulate himself that he anticipated a popular demand.

There have been several interesting articles in the magazines featuring the most popular patterns in fabrics, the most widely approved colors in carpets, draperies, upholstery, and paints. These are said to be the results of an analysis of nation-wide sales in the large stores and the statistical findings of paint manufacturers who mix colors to order. The editors interpret the answers to mean that the level of taste is on the upgrade, and from the pictures of attractive patterns and colors they seem to have made a cheeringly astute appraisal. The colors all harmonize and there is a nice variety. If the analysis is correct, everybody seems to be making the same choices. How does this miraculous supply-and-demand phenomenon happen?

The public has never created a specific demand; it is fashioned by manufacturers, designers, artists, and art dealers. The story behind the scenes goes something like this: a carpet manufacturer hires a "colorist" to develop a shade which is christened "Barococo." The same expert is employed by several other manufacturers and, fancying his new color, may use a dash of it in their products—drapery and upholstery materials. Thus a few important manufacturers feature "Barococo." When the small makers see the new lines of the big boys and the impressive ads plugging the new shade, they put it in their products too. "Barococo" is prevalent throughout the trade; even table linens and lamps, pottery and ceramics use it. *The color monopolizes public notice in many different designs and media.*

123

A few big manufacturers with a select collection of colors and designs, multiplied by the products of many small manufacturers using the same trends, equals the sum total of what is called "American Taste." It follows that anyone who buys the season's stylish patterns will want his paint job to harmonize and will ask for the color that goes with the palette of the season. There is no harm done, but it is misleading that the latest colors and patterns are insisted upon and publicized as the public's choice. They may become so in time, for better or worse.

When the work of an obscure artist touches a vital spring and overnight, like a jack-in-a-box, he pops up to the notice of a wide, appreciative audience, or when a style of furniture or art from a nearly forgotten past suddenly becomes "the thing," the public seems to be reacting as one. But the entrance of the star of the moment is not a haphazard event; it has been carefully contrived by a small group of practiced showmen.

The ways of producing a success are many. The work of an artist may attract the attention of a dealer, who gives him an exhibition; the critics are favorable; with promotion, the "art-conscious public" becomes interested. If the dealer is adroit he will purchase a number of the canvases for future speculation and concentrate upon making the artist's work generally known. He will secure exhibitions in other cities and other dealers' co-operation. If the artist has any personal eccentricities or can make sensational copy, or if his work has some characteristic that sets it apart, his recognition and success are speeded. His prices will rise each time he is given a prominent show, and inflation can be further hastened by auctioning some of his canvases. A few friends or interested promoters will bid them up. Seemingly overnight, the artist is "discovered." Eventually prominent collectors and museums may take notice and the dealer can unload the paintings he owns for a fancy figure.

Among the *cognoscenti*, pre-Columbian art has been avidly collected for some time. But the market is slowing up; the supply of good examples is lessening, and the merchants of art, who also depend upon the stimulus of new trends to lure new customers and interest old ones, are currently whispering that the aboriginal art of the Northwest, British Columbia, and Alaska will become the next collectors' enthusiasm. This is predicated on what some of the museums are acquiring, no doubt on what a few dealers themselves are picking up, and what discriminating art lovers are beginning to buy. If this trend catches on, anyone who knows what examples to choose can make himself a tidy wad by unloading at the top of the market. The public will wonder what brought it about and how a few were clairvoyant enough to anticipate its popularity.

The discerning public, which is the market for well-designed merchandise in all price brackets, has legitimate demands. Some manufacturers, store buyers, and salespeople are giving that public what it wants.

But what of the manufacturers, advertising pitchmen, factory salesmen, store buyers, and sales clerks who do not know the difference between good and bad design? These five groups of people, typifying thousands in the trade, are all gainfully employed foisting their indiscriminate taste on the final goat: those customers unable to judge for themselves, who must depend upon the recommendations of these tricksters of the trade. To spend money as they advise is like giving the gold cup in a better-baby contest to the mama with the most stentorian voice of praise for her progeny. Horace and his conspirators assert that he gives the public what it wants. They are wrong. His public doesn't know what it wants, what it's doing, or that it's being done.

Blasted into her role by the irresistible force of promotion, cozened from clubs and lectures, teased from luncheons and teas, a plump, pleasant, slightly muddled Hokinson lady exits from the elevator and bustles into a maze of mahogany, maple, walnut, and birch.

Now is the moment for which the trade has pooled its gargantuan effort. The customer has arrived to square the circle.

Mr. Artie Simpson caresses his tie, smiles a welcome. "May I be of service?"

This gentle phrase signals an epic meeting. These two people, like lonely suns whirling through the great galaxies of the universe, by a cataclysmatic, celestial calculus, converge.

Her eyes dart through the labyrinth of mismated furniture. "I'm looking for a table . . ."

"Traditional or Modern?" he asks, heroically throwing himself into the breach.

"Oh, not Modern!" she gasps.

Mr. Simpson steps briskly ahead. "Over here, please. Mahogany or maple?"

She looks perplexed. He fixes her with a steady eye. "Is your home formal or informal?"

She shuffles a riot of disordered mental pictures, the harvest of what she's read, heard about, and seen. "It's Provincial!" she produces triumphantly.

"Ah!" Simpson's eyes gleam with recognition. He moves a few graceful steps away, followed eagerly by the customer. "Dining or occasional?"

"Why—just a little table."

Affectionately he pats a small ornate contortion of mass-produced short cuts. "Here's a little beauty!"

Her eyes slide over it. "I'm afraid that's not quite——"

The salesman with the highest average in the store is undaunted. "I think I'm beginning to get a picture of your home! Mrs.—— I didn't get your name."

"Mrs. G. Magnon Crowe."

"Mrs. Crowe." He leads the way to a model room. "Look at this Three-in-One."

Obediently she does. A frown chases over her vague and placid countenance. "Is it Provincial?"

"Ah"—Mr. Simpson shrugs—"it's not *called* Provincial. It's part of the What-Ho Group featured on the cover of this month's *Well-Dressed Home.*"

This hits Mrs. Crowe where she thinks she lives. Though she is sure the Three-in-One is not the answer to her table problem, she examines it with renewed interest.

"It's no *one* style," Mr. Simpson amends.

Even to Mrs. Crowe this must be obvious. It is a disastrous compromise of several.

"Do you think it would do in a Provincial room?" she inquires hesitantly.

"It will go in any room," he replies, correcting her unfortunate use of words. "The Three-in-One"—he runs his hands over the top—"lamp or occasional table"—he slides a board out from it—"extendible tea stand"—he presses a hidden button and the front flies open—"there's your liquor cabinet!"

"Oh!"

"Your husband may not know periods like you do, but I'll bet he'll appreciate the hidden-libation feature."

"Well . . ." Now she is confused and tries to imagine how

her room would look with the What-Ho Three-in-One. . . . It's more money than George said he was willing to spend . . . No, better not. . . .

"I've been reading about Regency," she says from out of nowhere.

A faraway look comes over his face.

"They say it's the latest thing," she continues, gaining confidence.

He is silent, rapt.

"The magazines are featuring it for fall," she perseveres.

He switches off the dream; and, beginning to turn it into reality, "You don't know what a treat it is to meet a lady with your perception."

She dimples.

Almost tenderly, he escorts her to the grandiloquent display that Mrs. Crowe had missed on her trip in.

"Our newest promotion," he announces with impressive dignity.

She gazes at a "comprehensive" bedroom suite—a huge "Mr. and Mrs." chest, vanity with large mirror squatting between rows of picayunish drawers atwitch with elaborate hardware, two night tables, twin beds, a stunted chair, and draperies done in a peculiar shade of shimmering rayon-brocaded taffeta. Before the display a great blowup of an ad reads, "The Romance of Regency for Fall! We present BAROCOCO, *the* color of the season." The suite, a Louis-to-Adam-to-chance design in dark red mahogany, is highlighted by plenty of gilt and furniture polish.

Mr. Simpson rubs a loving finger over a tangle of bowknots on the chest. "Did you ever see more magnificent workmanship?"

Dazzled, she sighs, "It's beautiful——"

"You took the words right out of my mouth! Beautiful expresses it—beautifully!"

With an almost superhuman effort she glances away. "The—table I'm looking for . . ."

He smiles sympathetically. "We have to live with our furniture for a long, long time."

A small seed of panic begins to sprout. But like a sparrow hypnotized by a tiger, she murmurs weakly, "But—but—I mustn't think . . ."

He seems not to hear her. "If your home is suited to this exquisite suite—and I *know* it is——"

"But I have a . . ." Mrs. Crowe's voice drifts off as she thinks of the little scarred set in their bedroom at home—a makeshift bought when she and George were married.

"Traditional furniture, always in style, always smart, something you can live with, that can live with *you* forever." He takes out one of the drawers. "You know you love fine things," he says a bit chidingly.

"Yes, but——"

He turns the drawer upside down and reads from a gold heraldic shield, " 'The Lady Baltimore Gracious Living Group' —'Horace-Crafted.' That speaks for itself," he says just above a whisper.

Making one last desperate effort to escape, she backs away. "I don't think right now . . ." she says feebly.

"Why not!" Simpson demands exuberantly, blocking her path. "Why not treat yourself to something lovely! A fine set of furniture like this is not an extravagance. It's an investment, a hedge against inflation, an heirloom for the future!"

As Mrs. Crowe, now hopelessly mesmerized, examines each

piece she wonders what George would say. . . . Of course men have no taste . . . and resist change. . . . What a to-do there was when she fixed up his den, but he loves it now . . . and this would look so wonderful in their room . . . but it's an awful lot of money to lay out. . . . How grouchy he was about letting her buy one tiny table . . . Oh yes, the table . . . better go back and look for that . . . No. Why get something you don't really need . . . that's not economy. . . . Wait . . . George sold that lot on Elm Street. He's been talking about getting a new car! . . . And after all, this would be for both of them. . . . Why, when he got used to it, he'd love it. . . . Gracious living . . .

As Mrs. Crowe walks out of the store, bemused, smiling to herself, a little thrill of fear suddenly runs through her. What *will* George say?

A couple of nights from now, when George arrives bringing home the bacon, he'll notice something different, and in a belligerent tone will demand, "What's that?"

With commendable control she will reply firmly, "It's Regency."

The Cure

Someone once asked the late, great "Fats" Waller, "What is Swing?" He replied, "Boy, is you gotta ask, you ain't got it." Many people understand what good taste is in decoration and home furnishings—architects, designers, decorators, editorial personnel of magazines dealing with the subject; some in the wholesale and retail trade and a few customers. All these people are in general agreement about good taste. Their judgments are not arbitrary. They have an eye developed to appraise objects, and their assembly as a musician has an ear for a note in tune and a well-organized composition. They prefer certain things that appeal to them as individuals but are able to appreciate all things of honest design.

To explain good taste to those who know it requires as much effrontery as inviting a symphony conductor to listen to a scale.

But if "you gotta ask," you either haven't got good taste or don't know you have.

The quickest way to acquire it is to fasten your attention upon someone who has, watch what he admires and selects and find out *why*. This method is much like accompanying a judge to a few dog shows where pedigreed canines and promiscuous mixtures compete for the prizes. A few experiences in the ring and anyone could separate the aristocrats from the mutts. You might find, however, even after seeing why the judge awarded the blue ribbons to the champs, that you prefer plain purps. That's your peculiar privilege, but your time will not be wasted learning the difference.

Not everyone will be able to find a well-informed, indulgent friend or professional able to educate him to good taste, nor will he have the time or perhaps the interest to attempt a self-education program entailing some study of art, much reading, and attendance at galleries and museums. But because our surroundings exert a great influence on the kind of people we are, it is common sense to make them as good as our money can buy. If, after knowing the difference between the "dogs" and honestly priced and well-designed merchandise, you still like the mongrels, you'll have the courage of your eccentric convictions and the distinction of being one in a million, because those who know better choose the best. This fact is at variance with the unbearably hackneyed excuse, "Your taste may not be my taste," invariably mouthed by those whose taste is questionable.

There have been disagreements about taste ever since George Cro-Magnon, our original relative, stumbled out of the prehistoric morass and began to notice the little woman's attempts to civilize the cave. Nothing can stop it—if everyone had the best of taste there would still be personal preferences to pother about, and the home-furnishings trade would be just as busy catering to those. As a step toward a general basis of understanding and agreement, let us look quickly again at the influences we allow to confuse, mislead, and cloud our recognition of good taste:

Age is not an automatic measure of value. Whether an object is old or new, modern or antique, has nothing to do with its esthetic worth. It may be "of the period" or manufactured this year; only if it is good, honest design does it deserve your consideration.

A work of art is a work of art in any material. A beautiful material will not completely survive inartistic use and represents a poor investment intrinsically as well as esthetically. Look for decorative quality and good form first.

An out-of-ordinary method of manufacture is not a guarantee of extraordinary value; it has nothing to do with an attractive result. Any time spent on a poor effect is a waste. Don't perpetuate it by throwing your money away on anything whose appeal depends on the length of time spent or the travail of its fabrication. Forget how it was made and consider *why* it was made and if its reason for being is reinforced by its attractiveness.

A foreign stamp is no criterion of extra value. Travel cannot cultivate an inferior object; a distant land give distinction to the undistinguished. An import or product of home manufacture is important to you only if it is desirable in itself.

Costliness does not necessarily assure comeliness. You cannot afford an ugly thing at any price. Within your own budget—modest, medium, or munificent—fine things can be bought. If you collect rarities, the best buys are those that are both intrinsically and esthetically valuable. But when an object—that is not a rarity—is brazenly overpriced, you should be impressed only by the gall of the storekeeper, ineptitude of the designer, and blindness of the purchaser.

A master doesn't always create a masterpiece. The excellence of the interpretation means more than the signature. A piece with a pedigree may be an eccentric. The work of art is more important than the artist.

The relics of the renowned aren't always desirable. Greatness and good taste are not inevitable partners. An object bought for its story value may soon become a bore unless its colorful past is mated with good looks. The sensible reason for admiring or acquiring anything has nothing to do with the fame of its former owner but everything to do with its own decorative worth.

Overelaboration is not beauty. A thing may be remarkable for the skill of its craftsmanship, stunning effect, intricacy of design, and be as remarkable for its ugliness. Opulence is most often opposed to good looks.

The latest thing is not the best thing per se. Lord Chesterfield remarked, "Taste is now the fashion word of the fashionable world." Among many definitions, taste is said to be nice perception of artistic excellence, style, or form with respect to propriety, and etiquette. But style or fashion is the mere trend of the times, whim of the moment, or, more rarely, the necessity of the day, and can have much or little to do with things in good taste. Any suitable thing—well conceived and executed—popular or unpopular, from any period to the present, is worth buying. It is stimulating to watch the contemporary scene as fashions evolve and change, but to hail each new fancy with enthusiasm puts your back account in jeopardy. Wide appeal and general acceptance should not dictate your choices unless they happen to interpret fitness and good looks.

Emotional reactions, personal prejudices, and predilections do not point the way; to reach the right destination it is necessary to understand and appreciate the basic demands of good design to evaluate the esthetic worth of any object, then choose those that jibe with your personality.

It's crazy to try to live beyond your means—financially, culturally, or physically. You can't impress sensible people, whether they are above or below you on the so-called social ladder, by living in an unbecoming way, no matter how reckless it may be. And there's little point in showing off for your chums; if they've got all their marbles they'll figure you're a sucker; if not, they'll be on the same merry-go-round as you are, catching nothing but brass rings. And there's no satisfaction in being admired by a fellow chump. The things with which you choose to live should be expressive of you and suitable to the way you live.

There are worth-while things and many worthless ones on the market. You can't tell the difference by consulting the advertisements. It's up to you to make the proper choices. The trade puts a false value on many things not worth having. And since good-looking things are no more expensive to manufacture than eyesores, using good taste in the selection of home furnishings need cost no more and can cost a good deal less.

We have possessions for use, beauty, documentary reasons—intellectual, historical, archeological interest—and for amusement. The things that are merely for use, appeal to a documentary interest or to a sense of humor, are not always in good taste, but sometimes their characteristic quality is so interesting that they seem desirable. But generally the most important single quality is beauty. If a thing is not good-looking, it cannot fit our definition of good taste.

Ming pottery: at first shock this old chap seems about to blow his head off. A second look reassures. He is tenderly nursing a skin full of wine.

French table, c. 1800, with sensible shoes on little feet ready to walk off in opposite directio

138

. . . there's nothing like owning an elephant with mushrooms growing from his back . . .

Ivory balls: a lesson in technique and an amazing and amusing tour de force. First, a solid sphere with indentations; second, spheres spinning loose inside; third, the finished product: a sphere-within-a-sphere-within-a-sphere-within-a-sphere carved with vast intricacy and ornament.

Staffordshire Delft dish: William III, of
William and Mary fame, off for a placid
canter on his gentle mount with crown
and every curl in place.

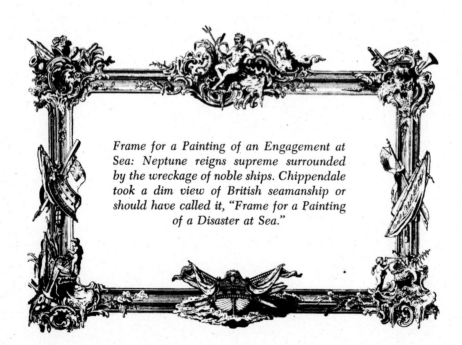

Frame for a Painting of an Engagement at
Sea: Neptune reigns supreme surrounded
by the wreckage of noble ships. Chippendale
took a dim view of British seamanship or
should have called it, "Frame for a Painting
of a Disaster at Sea."

140

"Functional" is a word nearly worn out by use today and employed to define the latest thing, the contemporary ideal, to interpret designs without any embellishment, stripped down to their skeletal essentials, to explain good looks and good taste and to excuse a plethora of bad design. The word means almost nothing or almost everything—all things of utility, all our household furnishings except purely ornamental objects, must function.

A viewpoint shared by many modern artists, designers, architects, and laymen is that "pure functional design," being as naked as possible and expressing basic use above all, is therefore the best kind of design. Does this recipe guarantee beauty? Gas meters, plumbing installations, and thousands of other things we see every day serve most useful purposes, are honest, simple designs. They are good expressions of mechanization and were never meant to be construed as anything else. But they have as much claim to good looks as some modern furniture and so-called decorative objects that give all to function and nothing to appearance.

If functionalism were "the thing" and it was carried to its proper conclusion, even our language would become basic—words of one syllable or grunts and signs would suffice for ordinary communication.

Some modern furniture considered the smartest by the functional folks has the same reasons for being as many of the elaborate jokes made during the times of the various Louis'. There are few chairs more accommodating to man's unnatural upright position than the posture chair used by typists. Its design has followed its function as have the designs of the most basic modern chairs. Why not use the posture chair in an exposed-member type of décor? Perhaps the open-sandal set would not

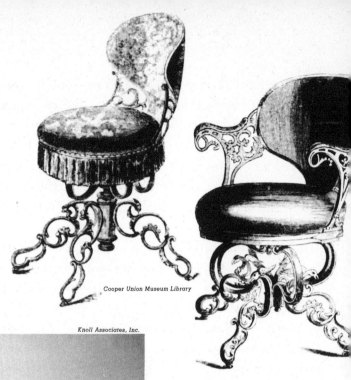

*. . . the posture chair
is no more ungainly than . .*

142

. . some of the nude cradles made for the posterior . . .

consider it smart or correct, but it is no more ungainly than some of the nude cradles made for the posterior.

Function does exist without beauty—and beauty without function—except that we may say that an art or decorative object's essential function is to be beautiful. Ideally that should be true; so should useful objects be attractive to look at and combine the two important qualities. But now let us think of use and beauty as separate ingredients. Consider for a moment the Father of your country and the gags and entertainments stemming from the suppositions that at certain houses, in those very beds, Washington once slept. There are few things more functional than a bed; if he slept well, good, and if the bed

143

is good-looking, splendid! Look at his desk. Whether or not he slept here is a matter for conjecture. It is functional, is it not? And is it not singularly unpleasing to the eye with its massive weight on such small legs? A historian or collector of Americana would find this document of early colonial days immensely desirable to own. But it would not be our choice.

. . . whether he slept here is a matter for conjecture . . .

Some illustrations of the functional:

Louis XVI writing table with convenient shelves for necessary materials, surmounted by candle-holders on the left for light and a clock to mark the passing hours.

Dressing table, original drawing by Hepple-white, who provided for every function from any angle for milady's maquillage.

144

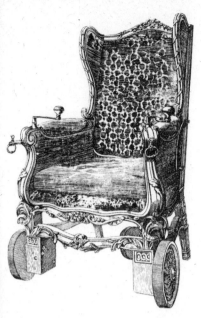

French mid-eighteenth-century self-propelling invalid chair, comfortable at rest or in motion.

Sixteenth-century Spanish vargueño—a desk whose front could be closed to make a handy chest, easy to transport from castle to castle with valuable documents intact and readily perused.

Louis XVI tub of luxurious embellishments and proportions—a forerunner of today's no-nonsense-plumbing-fixture.

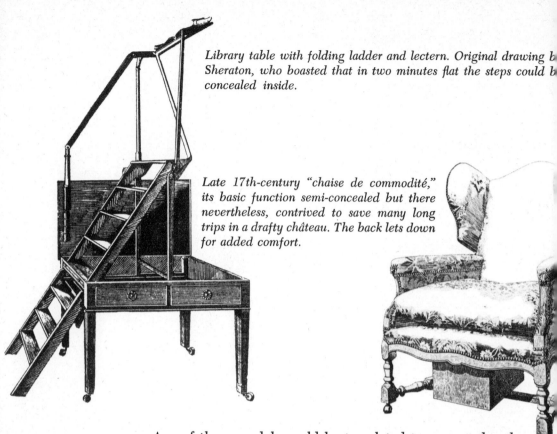

*Library table with folding ladder and lectern. Original drawing b[
Sheraton, who boasted that in two minutes flat the steps could b[
concealed inside.*

*Late 17th-century "chaise de commodité,"
its basic function semi-concealed but there
nevertheless, contrived to save many long
trips in a drafty château. The back lets down
for added comfort.*

Any of these models could be translated to present-day designs and serve their purposes no more admirably, though the results might be more attractive.

Everything in the house except purely ornamental objects must work—beds are to be slept in, chairs sat upon, chests used to accommodate things. If their appearance does not denote their uses, or denies them by the way they are designed, the eye will often find them vaguely displeasing and an emotional resistance will tend to alienate us from them. If they are flops in function but enjoyable visually, which is rare, they might as well be thrown out the window, and if kept around long enough will probably cause some such violence.

We needn't worry too much about "functionalism." There is still left in mankind so much of one savage trying to outcarve the savage next to him, one customer selecting a more elaborate knickknack than his neighbor, that the "basic boys" aren't likely to overwhelm us. Man's need of functionalism is too old to cause much of a revolution today.

There are no new basic-design ideas. But there are new ways of interpreting and adapting them, utilizing new methods and materials from fresh viewpoints. If the basic design is good, its readaptation and evolution often have a happy result. Good basic design usually springs from a reason for being.

Some basic designs can hardly be improved upon, so it is thoroughly reasonable to make exact copies of them today and enjoy their use in a decorative scheme suitable to them. But it is unreasonable to buy copies of period styles if they are a far cry from good basic design. Their lines have nearly always been changed to cut production costs. Their embellishments cannot be duplicated with the craftsmanship that decorates the originals. They haven't the beauty of patina age adds to wood. They nearly always look like the frauds they are. Certainly if a piece is needed to complete an authentic set, that is a sensible reason to copy an antique. Or if a fake is so clever that it fools the experts, and is a good design, make room for it. But with few exceptions, choose authentic antiques, well-designed modern pieces, rather than "period" copies.

A design may be elaborate and still be very desirable. But regardless of its surface embellishment, the basic form must not be unreasonably disguised. Bad designs are always the result of this misuse.

We do not deal here with trends, cycles of popularity, or attempt to predict the vogue or fashion, but point out that

147

certain designs were, are, and always will be good, good-looking, and in good taste. Perhaps the best interpretation of these basic designs has yet to be made, but as inspirations for thousands of adaptations—many good, many not worth notice—they are standards of excellence like the world's great books, not all of them to our personal reading tastes, perhaps, but admired for their true worth and with something for every taste.

There are no absolute rules for good design, and suggestions for its realization can best be seen. The basic designs illustrated can be found in countless variations—antiques from many periods as well as contemporary pieces. But unless some totally new methods of manufacture or new materials that make present ones obsolete are discovered, these designs will continue to serve as standards:

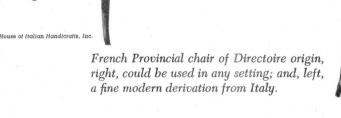

House of Italian Handicrafts, Inc.

French Provincial chair of Directoire origin, right, could be used in any setting; and, left, a fine modern derivation from Italy.

The Windsor chair, a favorite since the 18th century because of its strength and honest design. There are many variations for period and contemporary interiors.

Left, simple English country chair—oak, 18th century. Fundamentally an excellent design, it has been varied but never improved upon.

de and arm chairs from orth China, the bottom ngs made to raise the feet f the cold paved floors. though these are antiques, e curve of the backs and idth of seats add comfort to autifully proportioned, sim- e design, on a par with to- y's best expressions.

149

Left, original captain's chair. Center, the Douglas chair—a weste cousin of the captain's chair. Right, captain's chair in a mode variation. Originals as well as adaptations of this basic design nea all combine the virtues of comfort, good looks, and sturdiness informal rooms.

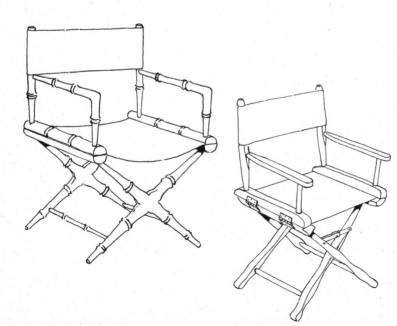

Folding officer's chair—i logical construction has le to several variations—on of these is the Chines Modern model on the lef

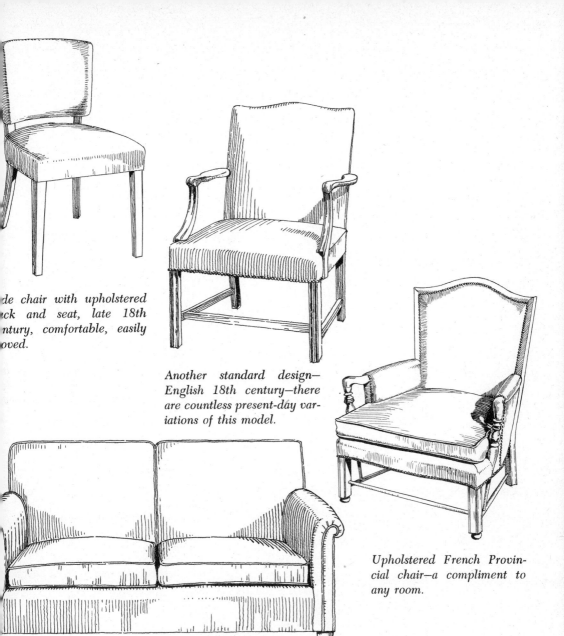

*de chair with upholstered
ck and seat, late 18th
ntury, comfortable, easily
oved.*

*Another standard design—
English 18th century—there
are countless present-day variations of this model.*

*Upholstered French Provin-
cial chair—a compliment to
any room.*

*The Lawson love seat. The same line adapted to chairs and couches
is generally associated with period furniture though it is not of antique origin. Upholstered pieces in many variations of this model are
appropriate in any interior.*

151

Wing chair, first used in 18th-century England. Though the function of the wings, protection against drafts, is not today's necessity, the feeling they give of shelter is part of the chair's inherent attraction.

One of its many variations—the poor man's wing chair used in colonial days.

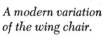

A modern variation of the wing chair.

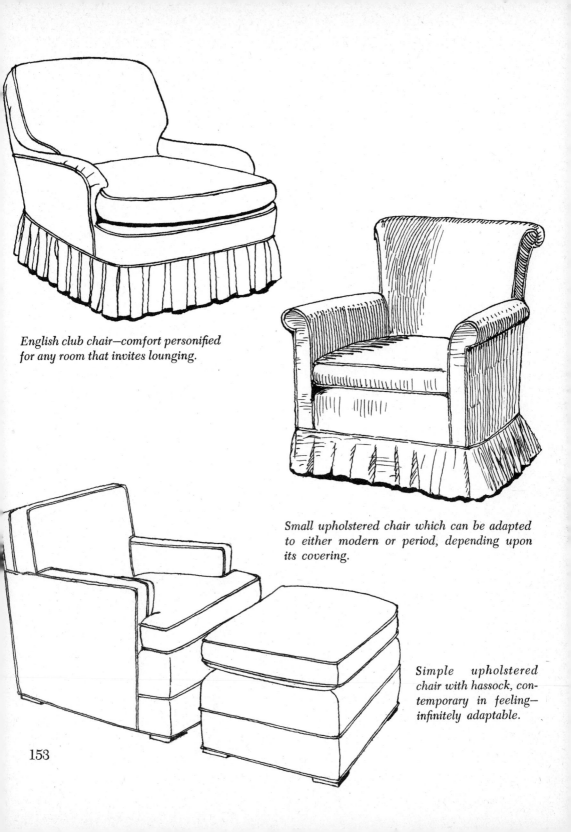

English club chair—comfort personified for any room that invites lounging.

Small upholstered chair which can be adapted to either modern or period, depending upon its covering.

Simple upholstered chair with hassock, contemporary in feeling— infinitely adaptable.

153

The Morris chair—its mechanical device that adjusts th
back from upright to lounging positions can be co
sidered a basic design. Sensible for comfort's sake, s
modern descendant happily adds handsomeness to fun
tion.

Sideboard, North China, a splendid example of pure,
honest design. The striking brass hardware a well-
placed contrast against the wood.

Pembroke table—late 18th century —modern versions are as practical as the originals.

Gate-legged table stemming from the mid-17th century. Modifications of this space-saving idea are used today.

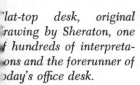

Flat-top desk, original drawing by Sheraton, one of hundreds of interpretations and the forerunner of today's office desk.

155

Trestle table, a design idea from which hundreds of variations have sprung. Gathering "round the board" probably first took place at a table like this.

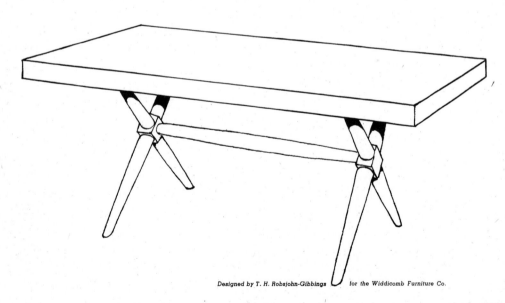

Designed by T. H. Robsjohn-Gibbings   for the Widdicomb Furniture Co.

156

French Provincial table from Alsace, a basic type like the trestle table, found from Scandinavia to Spain.

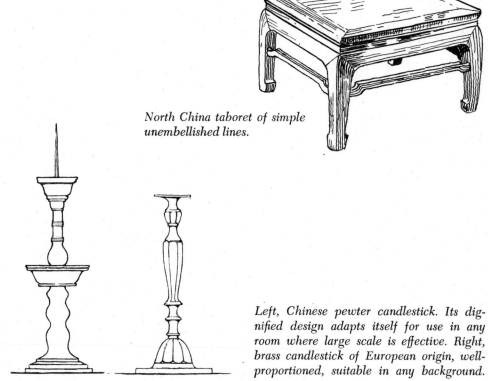

North China taboret of simple unembellished lines.

Left, Chinese pewter candlestick. Its dignified design adapts itself for use in any room where large scale is effective. Right, brass candlestick of European origin, well-proportioned, suitable in any background.

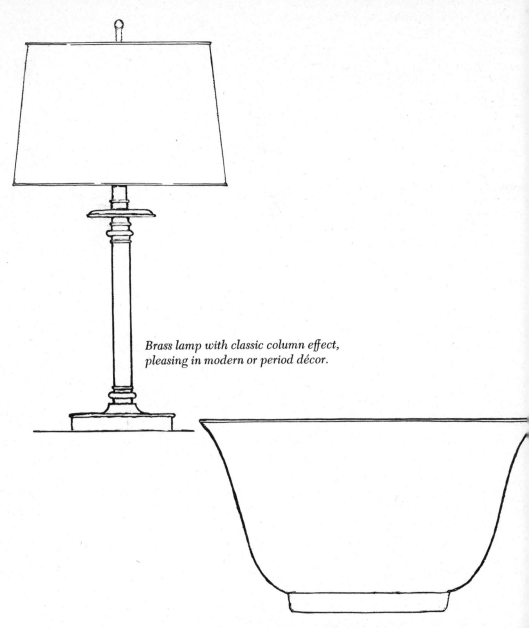

Brass lamp with classic column effect, pleasing in modern or period décor.

Chinese tea or rice bowl, the most basic shape of the Easte[rn] world. Familiar in America as early as the 17th century. Pa[ul] Revere admired its perfect form and used it as the inspirati[on] for the famous "Sons of Liberty" bowl.

Guernsey jug and Chinese tea-kettle—both antique in origin but so basic in design they appear to be modern.

159

Looking at these examples, it is obvious that from the standpoint of good taste categorizing is out. Certainly we prefer particular designs, we choose one style or period in preference to another. That's a nomination nearly everyone has already made, but if the election lies ahead, be sure your candidates stand on a platform of good looks.

Rarities—intrinsically and artistically valuable:

Jade birds: precious material used to its best advantage.
Only jade could give this effect of feathery, airy translucence.

*Sumerian steatite figure, c. 2100 B.C.
Strength achieved through stylization and
simplicity of form.*

*Chinese fisher-maiden: a delicate
masterpiece in coral.*

Greek bronze Sleeping Eros, c. 200 B.C. An angelic figure masterfully handled. Compare this to the "sensitive" sculpture on page 22.

Ivory figure: Chinese baby sleeping under a lotus, a simple, charming interpretation of a sympathetic subject.

162

Virgin of the Annunciation: French, 14th-century polychromed stone. A magnificent example of great Gothic sculpture.

Ming sculpture: its beauty of design and well-integrated mass resembles the Gothic in line, emotional impact, and decorative possibilities.

163

Greek bronze horse, c. 480 B.C. One of the greatest equestrian statues in existence. (It measures fifteen inches high.)

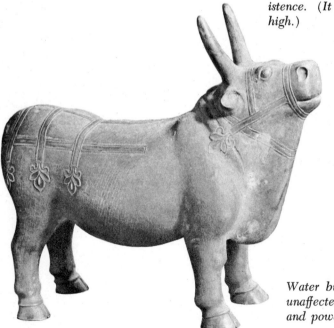

Water buffalo, T'ang pottery: A fine unaffected design expressing solidity and power.

164

An attractive assembly of good things is the final goal of good taste. Most books on design and interior decoration deal with effects and how to achieve them. So far we've confined ourselves to causes—how household objects come into being, mechanically and psychologically, why they should or shouldn't cross our thresholds, what to look for and enjoy, what to shy away from and shun. The assembly of things in good taste has been and is being covered by many excellent books, able lecturers, and worth-while exhibits. Often they explain the use of one type of decoration or art for a specific effect. Some of them recommend the congenial use of several periods in an effective manner—these are speaking our language. And in that idiom a few guides, warnings, and hints on how to make a house a home have their place here.

There are no available statistics on how many people are bored to death—at home. But there are plenty of studies made in offices, schools, workshops, and factories revealing that the use of interesting decoration helps to defeat absenteeism, low spirits, and inefficiency.

At odds with our sometimes simpleton actions are our complex natures and our individual twists and quirks. At this very golden moment there are scores of people reclining on couches in psychiatrists' sanctums, trying to cast their disordered psyches back to what caused the trouble. One of the fatal errors that sends us looking for help is the unreasonable repression of our individualities. We hasten to say if they would express themselves à la Lizzie Borden, repress them at all costs! But there are many harmless ways of expressing our complexities, and an important and rewarding one is at home. Shooting off steam in this fashion is not as popular as it should be—witness the same sort of contemporary interiors in thousands of houses and the stupid duplication, in detail, of period rooms. Those homemakers are neglecting a safety valve that might not only keep them out of a horizontal position at the psychoanalyst's but would make living more satisfactory and exciting.

If a friend dropped over one evening wearing knee breeches and a rash of lace at the throat and cuffs, we would hasten to summon the happy wagon. "Poor old Jim," we'd say, "slipped his trolley." But if he invites us into a room dressed entirely in the same period, no one raises an eyebrow. The detailed period habitat is no more wacky today than wearing the habit. It's playing Napoleon with the environment.

Someone else may declare, "I only like modern. Antiques, you can have 'em." And we pay little attention. But if he said, "When I travel, I only go to Oslo," we'd think he was a little soft in the filbert. Yet many entirely modern interiors reflect the same sort of limited viewpoint.

The unyielding sticklers for the modern and functional are as pretentious and ridiculous as someone with a one-track period complex who is Queen Anne queer. Those who insist that everything before the Bauhaus is bunk, in getting back to what they call "fundamentals," would ignore or toss out three quarters of the beauty of the past. Their enemies, a fence apart, who are no less sure that design stopped with Biedermeier, would pooh-pooh the progress and development of a world of wonderful things. Small-pasture jackasses, both of them.

Period was contemporary yesterday. Does real beauty change, time alter appeal, passing decades dim the desirable? Are Beethoven and Bach no good if Bartók is in favor? Did *Rain* drown *King Lear*? To love Shaw, must one hate Sheridan? Couldn't Jacopo Robusti and Picasso, Uccello and Utrillo, be

166

compatible roommates? Has a Bikini bathing suit got anything an Empire negligee lacked—if both are ideally filled? Would a juke-box Johnny spurn the Maja Vestada or—impossible to believe—the Maja Nuda? Not unless the decline of the human species is upon us.

We are all results of an evolution from many periods with roots in various countries and cultures, and as citizens of the United States a fine potpourri of many approaches toward living combined with a contemporary American expression. More than any other people, our tastes should be sophisticated.

Our palates are educated to gourmet's delights from many foreign kitchens and the vintages and spirits of the world. We enjoy all sorts of imported music, opera, drama, and literature. We mix them with enthusiasm and excellent effect.

No matter how well informed you may be on a certain period, how rich your knowledge of one country's expression, if you furnish a room entirely in that taste it will suffer from extreme ennui. The addition of even one or two contrasts of design will give sparkle, life, and individuality. A period room can be a wonderful background for modern paintings and primitive art. A modern room serves as a fine setting for antique paintings and decorative objects. Good contemporary furniture is complimented by the proper use of a few fine authentic pieces and vice versa.

The thirties saw the gradual decline—let us pray—of the "gilt complex." This was always an imported taste. Our founding fathers were flat, our early colonists were restricted by materials and circumstance. So now when the native American taste is beginning to jell—and it will be a long time before this hasty pudding becomes solid—our inspirations from early days are unaffected and our own times prohibit waste and recklessness.

Those who resist the popular trend toward simplification would modify their ideas if what they think of as "modern" were expressed in more elastic, pleasanter terms. They prefer period rooms because of the chances they afford for use of ornament and variation. But a predominantly contemporary room can be just as ornamental, interesting, and homey—with some mixture and elaboration of design. And a room with authentic period pieces, with a mélange of modern, can be as restful, easy, open, and inviting as a contemporary one.

The dividing line that separates proper elaboration of design and mad fancywork is one of the most controversial borders between good and bad taste. The struggle to define the point of demarkation has been the cause of more disagreements, even among experts, than any other factor of design. It is ridiculous to say that because the present trend is toward simplification, the less embellishment the better. This is true of the general taste today. But new trends are always coming along, and simplification will not necessarily stay in vogue indefinitely. Elaborate design may become popular again.

With the possible exception of the French Renaissance—an almost completely noxious period—every age has its good and bad examples.

. . . the French Renaissance . . .

. . . an almost completely noxious period . . .

168

Water pitchers, antique Irish glass.

Both collector's items, but the pitcher at the left is more valuable esthetically, a far more pleasing example of sensible shape and well-spaced cutting than its rarer and more costly companion—whose lines are contorted by the awkward base and ugly cutting at the top.

Spinach jade incensers: Right is an eye-popping example of artful crafts-manship in one of the most difficult materials to carve; but the less com-plex, less expensive one is a better work of art.

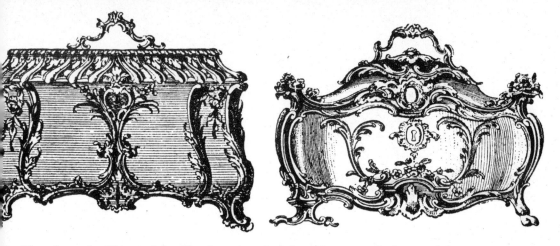

Silver boxes by Chippendale: The design on the left, with its straight lines and flat top, looks more stable and better balanced than the other with its bowed-in curves which would be more expensive to commission.

The chasing on the George II silver kettle follows its pleasing shape and, though it is elaborate, is generally very good design. Its style and proper use of ornament is much more desirable than the tea set whose basically good form is spoiled by unrelated chasing.

Rococo frames: A subtle difference here, but recognizable. The design on the right follows the rectangular shape of the frame, effecting a well-planned whole, while the other seems to fly off in all directions, disregarding the lines it should adhere to.

Primitive carvings: Here is a slight but important difference. Both have the same naïve decorative effect, but the figure on the left, West Central Africa, is superior. This uninhibited female has been carved just enough to retain the feeling of the original block of wood. For that reason its design is better than the Filipino—Igoroti—sculpture, which took more pains.

Ivory carvings, Chinese: These two lohans (disciples of Buddha) are both fine examples, but seen together, the one on the right is found to be superior. Its form is purer, its elongation makes it more graceful, the carving of the simple folds of the sleeves, the waistband, and the happy, serene expression are the work of a master, while its companion on the left is the work of a very capable craftsman.

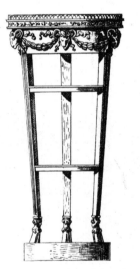

Grandfather clocks: The one on the left, Louis XVI, is in better proportion than the one on the right—Louis XIV. Both are excellent design examples of their periods. If the Louis XIV clock were shown alone, we would admire it, but by comparison, it must take second place.

Typical Louis XVI pedestals: On the left, we see straight supports, suitable garland and embellishment applied to a well-proportioned top, achieving balance and dignity. The faults of the other are apparent—bowed-in legs, turned-in feet, the weight of ornament, make it look distorted.

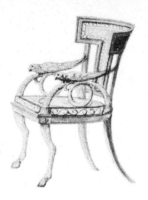

Chairs, French, c. 1800: On the left—an ill-conceived cross of bird and beast— seemingly the product of a nightmare or one absinth too many. The other chair, by the same designer in a more sober mood, was no doubt made for customers of modest means and good taste.

Cooper Union Museum

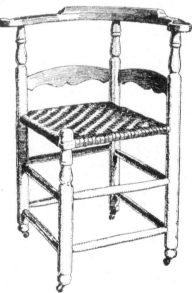

Corner chairs, Colonial or English: The example on the left is a valuable rarity and a crackpot design. The other, an ordinary corner chair worth far less, is better artistically.

Gothic chairs: The chair on the left has more stability of line; it honestly reveals the way it was made. The elaboration of the other disturbs the feeling of inherent structure; the tracery on base and back interfere with the conception of its design as a whole.

Louis XVI tables: The garlands, medallion, urn, and cupids which clutter up the table above seem unreasonable appendages, while the well-integrated, elaborate design of the lower table complements its good form and structure.

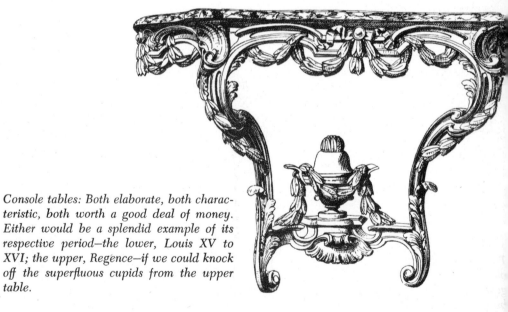

*Console tables: Both elaborate, both charac-
teristic, both worth a good deal of money.
Either would be a splendid example of its
respective period—the lower, Louis XV to
XVI; the upper, Regence—if we could knock
off the superfluous cupids from the upper
table.*

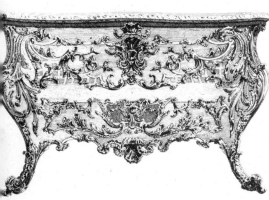

Louis XV chests: The chest at the left with its awkward shape, legs placed at a clumsy angle, and heavy, helter-skelter decoration is a farce compared to the one above.

The Louis XIV chest at right, with simple, straight lines, is another example of good use of decoration, with inlay and brass tastefully placed.

179

Louis XV desks: Above, is the desk that once belonged to the King himself. It is a masterpiece of cabinetwork and bronze ormolu mounts—as uniquely valuable as it is well made. Like a jewel that bedazzles but does not always adorn, it belongs in a special setting. But the other desk (by the same maker, Riesener), would be adaptable and becoming today.

Two rooms done at the time of the Exposition des Arts Décoratives in Paris, 1926. The room above was considered the last gasp in luxurious chic. Today it looks overburdened with design, "dated," and restless. The other, twenty-five years later, is still attractive.

Many young couples fixing their first nest find themselves with an assortment of wedding presents, mostly "modern"; a few things contributed by their families, of recent and ancient vintage; and their own personal treasured trinkets. What to do? How to tie together these modest prizes left on the altar of love? Make a few sacrifices—save up and buy that living-room suite for $350? Will that be the right start? Give a feeling of continuity to their simple abode? Perhaps, but it's likely that with a studio couch covered in attractive fabric, some unpainted furniture well finished at home with good-looking hardware added, inexpensive material of good design at the windows, planks and bricks for bookshelves, they can furnish their living room for less money in better taste. They will have nothing they feel they *have* to use until it wears out because it's an extravagance to replace a roomful of furniture which was so hard to pay for.

Whether you have a hundred dollars to spend or a thousand, assemble things for line, texture, color, and scale, not for one period, style, or category. Select good things of many periods— if they are compatible, use them together in any room, in any house. You can decorate in this fashion for little money, you will have a home that is uniquely *yours;* it will be much smarter, more attractive than the result of a lavish and careless use of money to assemble things that "all go together."

Here are a few general guides for combining complementary pieces of furniture, decoration, and art of all kinds.

Textures must be in harmony. Heavy country furniture and most contemporary styles look best with fabrics of rough weaves

—wools, coarse linens, nubby cottons; with decorative things of unaffected simple design.

Furniture with slick surfaces or elaborate design demands the opposite—finely woven fabrics or those whose textures and materials give a precise effect; decorative touches of refined and sophisticated design.

Scale must be in keeping. A small room with delicate details requires the same sort of furnishings. Large rustic rooms are suited to solid, bold decoration, to art objects with the character of Chinese tomb figures, pre-Columbian sculpture, South Seas carvings.

If a room is small, few colors should be used in the scheme. Variety can be achieved by nuances of the predominating ones and a few spots of a color in sharp contrast in small objects; this will make the room seem larger and give it a lift.

Large rooms should use more colors; bright, complementary ones keep large areas from looking like barns. In any sort of room the best effect can be achieved with one or two clear, true predominating colors with their opposites grayed.

Don't use ALL *pastel colors.* If they are preferred, let them predominate, but add touches of bright color in decoration or a high-key color in carpet, ceiling, or walls.

Control the use of pattern. Figured curtains, carpets, and upholstery all in one room give a restless and uncomfortable effect. Introduce pattern where it will be most telling and use plain colors for harmony and contrast.

Don't have everything plain, simple, monotone. This unenlightened habit has given contemporary décors a reputation for starkness and has steered thousands of homemakers away from modern decoration. The usual solutions for adding life to contemporary rooms are abstract paintings, or sculpture strategically placed, an area of wallpaper, or a mass of planting. Avoid them. They are clichés. Most modern furniture is plain, used nearly always against a severe background. There is not enough variety in strictly contemporary objects to make an all-modern room interesting; it needs the addition of things from other lands, from other days.

Don't match style, period, country, pattern, and design! Supply individuality by mixing the old and new, primitive and contemporary, the accepted and the unusual!

There is a striking characteristic shared by those with good taste: they are the first to acclaim worth-while new things. They have not become shortsighted from the habit of appreciating only what they are used to. We can get used to anything. Birds and beasts have learned to become accustomed to entering a red door to set off a mechanism that rings a bell which shoots the dinner into their cell. Soon these gentle friends of limited intelligence, who are obliged to suffer scientific experiments to secure the evening meal, automatically rush to the table, taste buds awash, whenever a bell rings—door, fire, or what not.

We are all creatures of habit alert to that which rings a

familiar bell. Be careful. Don't attend the trumped-up expensive nonsense dinned into your consciousness by the power of publicity. The market abounds in frauds, fancies, and fine things. Get in the habit of looking for your taste in good design in the world's small shops and great stores. Always remember good taste costs no more!

Designed by Alma Reese Cardi

Composed and bound at Country Life Press, Garden City, N.Y.

Printed by Kipe Offset Process Co., Inc.